Naibhu
A Spiritual Odyssey

Naibhu
A Spiritual Odyssey

Valerie V. Hunt Ed.D

Copyright © 1986, 1998 by Valerie V. Hunt.

ALL RIGHTS RESERVED

NAIBHU, A Spiritual Odyssey is fully protected under the copyright laws of the United States of America, The British Empire, including the Dominion of Canada, and all other countries of the Copyright Union. No part of this book may be reproduced by any means including recitation, lecturing, public reading, radio broadcasting, television, cable, video cassettes, audio cassettes, and any other means of copying or duplicating. All rights, including the rights of translation into foreign languages.

Publisher's Cataloging-in Publication
(Provided by Quality Books, Inc.)

Valerie V. Hunt
   NAIBHU: a spiritual odyssey / Valerie V. Hunt – 1st Ed.
   p. cm.
   ISBN:0-9643988-4-2

   1. Spirituality. 2. Spiritual life. 3. Past life readings. I. Title

B841.H86 1998   291.4
                         QB198-81

Published by:
Malibu Publishing Co.
P.O. Box 4234
Malibu, California 90264
Printed in the United States of America

Chapter One

    From the view atop a camel the land that slowly passes is gentle rolling hills covered with fields of waving grain, native to the land. At times as the land drops away—hazy in the distance rise the great foothills of the Himalayas—and beyond occasionally a white topped mountain rises so high it appears as a piece of cloud—not attached to the earth. Small rocky ravines gouged out by the rushing snow waters split the fields. Goats clamber over the rocks and spill out into the grain land. Many colored goats attract a small boy perched on a wooden frame astride a camel.
    This slow moving caravan of camels, horses and yaks started in China—they are coursing the merchant trails west. It stopped a few days earlier in Kashmir to pick up fresh animals and merchandise. Now it is headed for Old Persia with only sparse settlements between.

A small boy is passively restless from long days of sitting on this rough animal. His mother rides on another camel with a canopy over her head. Only women and small children ride—the men walk and command the animals. Although the days are long, there are occasional stops to rest and water the yaks at springs coming from the rocks. The little boy is always restless from sitting so long and still; he is unhappy to have left his home in Kashmir. As the caravan stops, he asks a man to help him get down. No one else alights. He runs around behind the animals for a short distance from the trail. A bit farther he sees a pile of huge rocks and boulders with openings and crevasses—a perfect place to play. He runs as fast as he can to explore them. He has not played for days. Further, nothing has peaked his curiosity like these powerful rocks. He creeps through tunnels through shafts of light and dark, imagining what he will see next. He is lost to the joy of his imagined world. Nothing matters, his sadness is gone and he can just be a child again.

When he finally comes to an opening pointing west he looks down at the trail and caravan to see that it is barely visible in the distance; it has moved on without him. He runs after it panic-stricken and screaming, but no one hears him. The caravan continues into the distance. He walks around. He doesn't know where he is except it is a place where his caravan stopped to get water by some rocks. When his people replenished their water, they went on without noticing that the little boy was gone. Apparently only the man who took him down from the camel knew that he had gone off to play. Later in a haste to redirect the animals, this man had forgotten.

The little boy looks off to the east where he sees some dust rising. He believes that someone is coming back to find him and deliver him back to his caravan. When the caravan arrives, it passes him without stopping. He screams for their attention. He almost gets trampled by animals trying to stop them, but they keep on going. He thinks that they see him, but they do not stop. That goes on for a long time; caravans pass and no one stops.

At this time he is a very little boy about five years old. He knows he lived somewhere in Kashmir in a nice house; he had a lot of playthings. There were servants who took care of him. His father was busy with people. His mother, whom he didn't see very often, was beautiful, a tall stately woman with olive skin and dark hair and eyes. She belongs to a high family from Persia. On this particular journey, she was taking the boy back to her people.

Here among the rocks at the side of the trail he has nothing, no parents, no servants, no playthings and no house. He does not know where he is. He does not know what to do or what direction to take. So he just stands there beside the trails. As it gets dark, he is very, very afraid. There is no protection anywhere except the rocks that he loved to play in. Still very upset and slightly panicked, he goes back to the pile of rocks, searching for the best hiding spot. What seemed so exciting in the daylight becomes foreboding at dusk. He finds the smallest niche where he can force his body—where big things cannot enter. But he cannot sleep. Neither does he weep. All his senses are alerted. Suddenly, a mysterious, beautiful lady seems to come to hold him. She lights his fearful little crevice, and her gentle warmth makes him forget. He sleeps.

He awakens in daylight—amazingly calm but very hungry. He is disoriented and confused about where he is and how he got here. The "lady" appears again just as he is about to run or cry. He sees her for sure, but she does not look like his mother. She drifts around and doesn't seem to walk, She says she will show him how to live in this wilderness. She takes his hand as they walk into the hills. He has played games like this before in his imagination when he was alone. So despite his hunger and the increasing roughness of the ground, he forgets his discomfort and is lost on this beautiful journey. They come to a new valley sunk deeply in rough hills. Below on grasslands he sees a large herd of goats. He rushes toward them as if ignited. The goats too seem to recognize him and surround him like old friends. The beautiful lady disappears.

That night the little boy sleeps with his new goat friends. Somehow they know he needs them desperately. He is like another goat kid who nestles closely to their bodies. It seems easy for him to accept the comfort and protection of these living things. Later he will know that they were his first teachers to make this extraordinary life possible.

In the days to come he stays close to the goats, never straying more than a short distance. He watches them intently and constantly. He seems compelled to see and know all about them. He has never had a close animal friend. His mother objected, and although he had seen goats, he never had a chance to run his fingers through their soft hair, feel their hard heads and their slender sinuous bodies. He touches the goats a lot and they like it and come to him for more. He watches them eat the tender grass shoots. He tries eating the grass, finding it bitter but somehow satisfying. He watches the baby kids suckle enthusiastically; they seem contented when they finish. He tries suckling also and finds it good. In the first days he suckles many mother goats. His need seems intense. In each instance, the goat mother accepts him like her own. The colors fascinate him as they flash in the sunlight. The birds awaken him in the morning and late in the evening; he closely watches them swooping and darting so gracefully he feels himself being like them.

Each day he ventures a bit farther down the valley. The excitement of new discoveries keeps him ever alert. When he wanders too far, the goats move toward him to assure him of their concern. Each evening the whole group returns to one area where they sleep.

He chases the baby goats and runs with them trying to jump as high as they do. When he falls, they lick his face and climb onto his shoulders. He loves these playmates. Never before has he had so many living playmates. The sun is warm and the grass soft for frolicking and always his living friends surround him.

Each day he learns more. He sees little crawling things and follows them intently for hours seeing what they do. He watches squirrel-like animals in the rocks carrying things they had dug from the ground. He follows to find how and where they dig their prizes. He spends his days learning, sleeping and hunting things that taste good. The animals show him what to eat, and always when he is hungry, a nanny obliges him with rich strong milk. He is never denied. They give him food, protection and a family of living, breathing beings. He studies how they all care for the little ones; he watches the behavior of the leader of the group. They love the rocks and climbing places that he has difficulty following. But he struggles and eventually gets up to the top. He is thrilled to see so far, such a big world. These goats seem very special to climb so high to just see and imagine what is beyond. He climbs daily with them because up there he sees the beautiful lady and she loves him and comforts him.

His days are full. Full of physical things he learns to do by watching animals. His days are rich in the sounds that he hears. Birds and chirping things immediately attract him. When the goats alert, he does too. He hears what they hear and he always finds the source of where the sound comes from. Sometimes it is days later, but he persists. He is aware of intense colors that seem stronger than he had ever known. The sparkly colors in the rocks put him in trance, particularly on warm days when the heat from the rocks cause him to melt into them. One part of the valley is moist from water trickling from under rocks, there the flowers grow profusely. He lies down to watch the bugs and see the iridescence of each petal. He tastes flowers and likes them, some are sweeter. The birds show him a gray-blue berry on a scrubby plant between rocks. He thanks the birds for he loves these. He eats all he can find. The orange berries on bigger bushes make him a bit giddy as these do the birds, but he likes the feeling. This little boy grows rapidly, and becomes agile as the goats, strong and daring. His mind is full of his learnings. He wonders if he will ever know as much as his animal friends. He finds seeds in the summer by watching birds. These are a rare treat for him and they fill his stomach fuller than the grass, berries and roots.

He is cold at times, particularly when it rains. The goats do not seem to mind but he does. His need drives him to look for a shelter among the rocks. The first niche he finds doesn't work, for the rain comes from another direction and fills the niche. The next place that he finds the rain runs away and leaves it dry. He fills it with dry grass; the goats sleep in the entrance and he stays very warm.

This boy seems to have forgotten his earlier life. It is as though he belongs here, is a part of the natural scheme of things, so his needs are fulfilled. He does not remember his parents or Kashmir. He only knows he is alive, strong and loved by his goats. His life is an exciting and very real adventure; each day is full of new discoveries. He never thinks about tomorrow or what he is to do later in his life when he is full grown. His life and all his attention is for now. Some natural force and knowing is with him constantly. When he feels a touch of sadness, the "beautiful lady" comes down and radiates him.

Chapter Two

    This little goat boy lives in the fields of this beautiful valley for about five years. In the winter time the goats come down the mountain to lean-to sheds where grain and hay are provided. He comes with them. As long as he is with his goats, he is a relatively happy little boy. With his survival assured, he has time to dwell with spiritual images. The beautiful lady is with him often.
    One year, when he is about ten, the men come up to get the goats to put them away for the winter. Although they had seen him before now, they wanted to take him farther below to work with the yaks. He is big enough now to care for the big animals. He doesn't really want to leave his goats but something tells him to go, that he needs to be with humans.
    Reluctantly, he follows two men who are the owners of these big goat herds. They take him to a barn-like

structure where there are a group of men who care for a large bunch of yaks. This is a strange experience for him because he hasn't been around people for five years. He only occasionally saw the owners and never communicated with them. By this time, the little boy has forgotten his own language. He has not spoken words since he became a goat boy, but he is bright. He listens, he watches and he understands. However, without language; he appears dumb. These men are teaching him to take care of the yaks. But they are very crude and loud men, and he does not feel comfortable at all. They make many demands upon him. He just runs all day long, serving their needs so that by nightfall he is very tired. He falls into the hay bed at the end of the barn above the yaks. There is no peace and quiet like there had been up in the green valley. They give him cooked meat to eat and it makes him sick. His stomach is always upset from yak butter and meat! They cook everything, and he is used to raw things. The tastes are strange and sour. He doesn't feel very well and is unhappy. The men bang him around roughly in jest, but it hurts. He watches. He watches intently. He works with the yaks and a few camels.

He likes the yaks best; the camels are mean. He does not know what he is going to do but he isn't happy; he wants to go back to his goats, but he knows the men will bring him back here. He is bigger now and he can work more. The men drink a lot — some black looking stuff. They are loud at night. He does not sleep well. He moves to the outside of the barn-like structure because the men sleep inside, and he is apprehensive around them even when he is awake. One night he is asleep and the men are out celebrating. When they come back, they are loud and drunk. They stumble around the barn and pull him from his bed. He is scared of their wildness and their big "cocks." He senses they are going to play with him and hurt him. He is very upset. He does not really know what is happening, but he senses it is not good. He squirms, jerks and slips away from them because they are drunk.

They are not very coherent, and they cannot move very well so he slips away easily from their awkward hands. He runs to the end of the barn and he vomits. As he continues running, he vomits and wretches more. He heads in a northeasterly direction. He wants to return to his goats but he knows he cannot because they will find him there and bring him back. It is the middle of the night. He cannot see where he is going but he is running north east.

He travels for several days, mostly east... slightly north until he comes to a desert area. It is not as mountainous or rocky as where he had been with his goats. It is not a pasture like it had been with the yaks. It is kind of a rocky desert. There are things growing but not very well. He finds a cave and he crawls in, sore, tired and upset. He has hardly stopped running since he left the barn. There isn't any sign of habitation. He knows nothing about the desert. The things that he had learned in his little valley, what to eat and where to go, don't seem to apply here. Again he is lost. All he knows is to stay in his cave because it is protection.

The next day he starts out to roam, seeing what is around and finding food. He eats some cactus pods; these don't taste good or set very well, but they do curb his hunger. He surveys the dry valley. There are some houses down there. In fact, there are a number of houses—more than he has seen. He decides he will return at night because he can be seen in the daytime. Somebody might take him. Somebody might do something with him. He decides to take a look after nightfall when it is quiet.

He takes off again in the dark into the valley toward the village. He sneaks around to see what is here. There is nobody around but there are some animals. He wanders around to find out where everything is kept, to get the lay of the place. He steals some grain. He knows he has a source now. He can steal and not go hungry. He can survive this way until he gets bigger and older; then he will find some work. When he gets big enough, he will go into the village openly and they will not know where he came from. Then, nobody will take him. He has found a home in his cave, and he is going to live there until he was big enough to go elsewhere. Then he could work. He enters an old barn-like structure and finds some yaks inside. He steals an old blanket and a torn piece of cloth. He returns to his cave happy.

Every night he goes into the valley. He sleeps all day and he prowls all night; nobody sees him. He learns where everything is stored in the village. He knows when people are going to be there and when they aren't going to be there. From his cave he seems to "tune in" and know where everything is. He can particularly tune in to where the food is kept and where he can safely get to it. He takes just a little bit; he doesn't steal more than he can carry or eat. He just takes enough.

It seems that the young boy is always hungry; he is cold and starved. He sneaks into a house while the people sleep. He is very stealthy. He steals cheese and dried meat, but he looks for anything that he can eat. He steals some clothes too, something to keep him warm because he is always cold. He doesn't try them on—he just takes them back to his cave. The young boy is starting to have real trouble because he feels unprotected. The beautiful goddess doesn't come anymore; he is far from the goats and he feels all alone. When he was up with the goats, he was never alone. He had his goats and he had the "beautiful lady" too. He had all kinds of beings that took care of him. He is no longer small, and so there is no one to protect him. The more he steals the more endangered he feels. He has deep sadness about this.

He thinks about going into the village in the daytime to let some kind person know somehow that he wants to work, to help with the yaks. He is constantly afraid of people because he cannot talk—he doesn't trust anyone. He is afraid that he will be taken back to those men, so he chooses to live in this cave alone. Something is happening to this young boy which is very exciting to him. He seems to forget about his hunger, his coldness and his needs because he is changing. He doesn't like what is happening. Some days he stays in his cave. He thinks about the "lady." He thinks about the goats. He thinks about beauty and the birds and the love of animals he used to watch, when everything was lovely. His stomach begins to hurt so badly and he feels so cold; he becomes angry and he returns to the village to steal. He could have stolen money, but he could not use it. This village is made up of people who handled animals for the caravans that came across—the international caravans, the caravans from India and from China. They went to the Near East and brought things to Europe and to Greece and to all that land. This little village supplies animals.

He begins to have intense internal struggles. The conflict is between what he believes and what he is doing. The beautiful times in his life are less and less; he lives like a hermit. He finds water and he steals. That is his life. He is never caught although he becomes more and more bold. As he becomes more sure of himself, he ranges farther and farther. He is traveling south. He walks most of the day to see what is there. He keeps stealing more things, some knives. He steals an image of an old, old man...very interesting. It is an old man's face carved out of stone; the man's face so intrigues him that he had to steal the carving. He puts it in one end of his cave with the knives that he stole. He generally doesn't take a knife when he leaves the cave unless he is traveling vast distances.

The farther south he goes the more often he comes to the international trail crossing this land. He sees fires. He waits till dark; then he goes down and has a look. There are tents, so he looks inside. He is afraid to go inside the tents, but he looks. He sees all kinds of things in the tents that he has never seen before. All kinds of things that came from....he doesn't know where. These things intrigue him. He wants to touch them. He wants to be with them. He never saw anything like these things in the barren houses up in that little village where he had been. There was nothing like that. All sorts of things are kind of spilling out of pouches and bags. He loves the smells! The smells are extraordinary. Everything seems to fascinate him. He enters the tents a little ways and then he goes away. He finds that he can creep in very quietly and steal the food in the tents. However, he doesn't recognize most of the food. It doesn't taste anything like what he is used to. It is a kind of bread that is doughy and sticky and strange. Some tastes are sharp and make him grimace. He isn't used to things like these, but they fascinate him because they are new and they are food.

He steals some very pretty things because he wants them. He wants them in his cave. He wants something very beautiful to set the little carved head on. One night he steals a magnificent, big, heavy, rough and coarse kind of blanket. He steals this blanket to take it back to his cave. It is so warm that he likes to lie on it. He steals something that is bright and has sparkly things on it. It is thin and is gold. He puts it in one corner of his cave and drapes it around the rocks. The sculptured head is put up on the top so he can sit and look at it. This man is very special. Staring at this carved head made all of the dullness and all of his sadness disappear. He steals a metal pan with a wick and oil which he puts beside the little old man to light his face. He sits and watches the glow and he dreams until the oil is gone. He dreams that he is sitting inside a magnificent place.

He goes less and less to the village. The stealing is too good at the camel caravans. It only takes him part of the day to reach the trail and he is back by morning. He goes down in the afternoon and waits...he does his stealing then he comes back under the cover of darkness. No one ever knows. No one ever imagines. The caravans move on the next day so there is never a problem.

He gets bolder and bolder. Instead of just going in and taking what he can easily see, he decides to have a look around. He can only carry so much, but he will select what he wants. Not just anything...he takes only food and things to make his cave beautiful. He takes things to look at and to wonder about. He's never seen things like these. It is like another world is coming in—a world that is somehow connected with caravans.

He spends less time in the wilds. He doesn't have to go search for his food anymore. He knows where it is. He is stronger. He can carry more; so he carries back enough to last him several days, so he doesn't have to go daily. He takes a little bit from each tent, so nobody knows.

One night he is feeling particularly bold and carefree as he approaches a huge caravan. The tents are more numerous and larger than the others. He chooses the biggest one, a very special tent that has some decoration on it. It is black and has some shiny things hanging down. He goes in. There are three men sleeping inside; they are big men. When he sees them, he does not like them. He doesn't like their faces as they sleep. The only face he likes is that man—that stone figure that he had stolen in the little village.

He is rummaging around less quietly in his excitement when one of the men awakens. He kills him by cutting his throat as slickly as you could imagine. He runs quickly leaving everything behind. No one else awakens. He slits the man's throat from one side to the other, all the way from ear to ear, like they did with slaughtered goats. He has absolutely no feeling. That man would have caught him and killed him right there. That would have been the end of him. He runs quickly back to his little cave. He looks around and when he sees his statue, he weeps.

Chapter Three

He stays inside the cave for days. He doesn't leave and he doesn't sleep. He continuously relives the experience of sudden, explosive killing, of slyness and the great surge of power that had come over him before he killed. He came back to his cave eager to rest with the beauty he had created there. Instead he is distraught. He doesn't understand nor does he know what is happening to him and he doesn't know what to do about it. He goes back and forth between intense guilt, anger and rage ending in an urge to kill. He wonders if maybe he could have outrun that man instead of killing him. Something had happened and he had wanted to kill him; he killed out of brutality, not self defense. His suffering is intense. He doesn't know which way to turn; he is absolutely torn.

He goes into a kind of shock state making it

impossible for him to think any more. This brings some peace. He tries to find the "beautiful lady" but he cannot find her. He tries to imagine himself with his loving goats, but he cannot see them. He spends several days in this stuporous state. When he recovers sufficiently to know, he realizes that a major choice has been made and that this choice will dictate his life's direction.

He is hyper alert. He knows that he can have anything that he wants because he can steal it. He feels very powerful; he is strong; he is skillful. He doesn't care about people; he will live as he wants to live and he will take what is needed to make it so. He is joyful. He has found a way that will end his struggles. He had previously thought that when he was older he would go down to the village and walk in as if he had been wandering. He would go in and get some work. There he would live and care for the animals for the rest of his life. Now he knows that he will never do that, not ever. He will be a part of the gold and the glitter he has seen. He will have comfortable things like his blanket.

He is a teen-ager now...a big teenager, strong and agile. He doesn't know how huge he is. He has never stood beside another man. He has only seen them from a distance. He is still highly skilled in surviving with nothing. He knows how to live on berries, seeds and grass...he has learned how to protect himself from the rain and the cold.

He is again on the international caravan trail stealing food. He doesn't hunt for food anymore; he knows where to find it. He returns to his cave in the early mornings, tired. He brings enough food to last a few days this time. He has stolen a few baubles, but he saw many more, too many to carry.

When he returns to his cave he finds it barren. While he was out stealing, his cave was stripped clean of all of his possessions; they are gone. His first thought was that he is in the wrong place. He looks everywhere for his magnificent blanket and cannot find it anywhere. His prized possession, a big black and white blanket with its bold pattern, is gone. His statue, which had been sitting on a gold cloth in a small cove in the wall is gone too. His home is gone; only the cave remains. He realizes that he has been found out. He knows that he must leave quickly; to stay until morning would be too dangerous. He reassembles his stolen food and heads for the village in the dark. He is determined to discover who has found him.

Quietly he enters the house where he had stolen the old man sculpture. He spots his possessions, the gold material, the sculpted head and his precious blanket. He gently picks up the statue. He doesn't need the other things, only this, for he must travel lightly.

He leaves the village not knowing where he is going. He is very sad. Recently he had not been content with the cave, knowing that it was only temporary. When he first moved in, he was too little and too young to get a job. He suspected the people would have abducted him or abused him so he bided his time in the cave. Now he is a robber and a killer; he has been found out. Someone knows where he lives though they have never seen him. No one has ever seen him. They do not know what he looks like; he does not know what he looks like either. He has never really looked at himself.

He rapidly heads northeast despondently. He is constantly trying to figure out what to do or some way to change the things that are wrong. He tries to think. He doesn't want to keep stealing. He wants other choices. He cannot ask for help because he has forgotten his language. Actually he does not trust people; he trusts only animals. The only woman he remembers is the "beautiful lady" but she can't be called upon; she comes without warning.

The robber boy is nearly twenty years old now. For days he has moved steadily eastward. He abandoned the northern direction because it took him too far from the caravan route. He doesn't like the land very much; there are bigger rocks and more mountains here. Every few days he goes south to keep touch with the caravans and replenish his food supply. He takes nothing else. He continues to be sad. Nothing has changed in his life except that now he knows he is hunted. Things don't improve while he is traveling, but he has no choice. His mind is constantly busy thinking. He doesn't have a language and no real skills except survival skills. He has the urge to run away—to where, he does not know. He is always running. He wants to go to some place where no one knows him. How strange, no one knows him anywhere. He has no identity.

He finds an old man alone where there are no caravans, a place that seems apparently barren of human activity. In the early morning light, he sees the little old man beside the trail hunched over as if in pain—probably he is very cold also. The cold increases as the land becomes higher and the mountains loom in the background. He approaches the old man not sure if he is alive. After observing the old man for some time, he touches him gently. The old man stirs and raises his hairless head to peer at Naibhu with watery eyes sunk in deep sockets. An ancient weathered face with so many lines makes the young man wince at this almost inhuman expression. Apparently the old man has been cast aside from the caravan as worthless.

This is the first human he has consciously chosen to relate to during all of those years of his solitary life. A strange feeling occurs when he discovers himself as a separate human from this old man. A realization that somehow connects him to humans, an identity that seems far away but real.

He remembers his name is Naibhu. He had never totally forgotten it, but names are only important when relating to other people who also have names. Goats and birds and other living things know him in other ways and not by that kind of language. "Naibhu," "Naibhu," has a ring that he recalls, but he doesn't speak it. He has lost the capacity to talk. This is the only word he has and it is a precious tie to his past. He is somebody.

Naibhu picks up the old man and carries his frail

body up toward the hills. His impulse is to dispose of the ugly, old man rather than to save him. He feels no compassion of love or any tender feelings. He thinks, however, that if he saves the old man he might learn to speak. The old man mumbles, so Naibhu figures that he has a language. As they move into the hills, Naibhu looks for a cave, a place to live for a longer time. He is accustomed to living unprotected; there is no trace of memory about living in a house, but this old, sick man might need some cover from the cold nights.

The land gets rockier but without caves or niches. The skinny load on Naibhu's back gets heavier with his failure to find a shelter. Finally, he stops beside some large piled up rocks where people cannot easily see them. He sits there and holds the old wizened one who is very sick. Some compassion returns as it had so often when he tended sick goats. He holds the old man much of the day, feeding him slowly from his stolen food. Naibhu thinks this old one will be a real liability. Where he had been free to run, now he has the responsibility for an old man, to feed him and to nurse him.

The healthier the old man gets the more he complains. He does not like the food, the bed and the cold. Naibhu is very unhappy with him. He grumbles all the time. The more time Naibhu spends trying to take care of him or helping him, the more irascible the old man becomes. Naibhu thinks he might learn to speak from the old man. He speaks often now, almost constantly. Naibhu gestures to the old man to slow down his speech, but the old man speaks faster and faster and Naibhu does not learn. He brings food for them; he steals from the caravans and the old man wants all the food. Miserable old coot, he wants it all! The young man is willing to share generously with the old coot, but he is not willing to give him everything. Naibhu doesn't trust the old man. He is afraid to go to sleep around him, so he leaves him in the rocks and climbs up farther to sleep alone.

One night on his caravan forage, he steals fabric for a

small tent. As soon as he assembles the tent at his hiding place, he realizes that it is easily seen from a distance because of its bright colors. He discards it. Again he has nowhere to hide. This makes him restless, but he is tied to the old man.

He begins to sleep by day and prowl at night. He now visits the caravans, not to steal but to watch and learn from the shadows of people. He watches the men around the campfires but from a distance, so they cannot see him. It is as though he wants to know what the world is like and these people are his only source. He does not know anything. He knows he is searching for some other way of life about which he has no information at all.

Chapter Four

   The old man begins to walk; soon he is running around, snooping everywhere. Naibhu never lets him know when he is leaving; he never tells him where the food comes from; he never talks to him at all.
   Each morning Naibhu returns to his pile of rocks, a formation with alley ways and crevices to hide in. One day he comes back to find three new men that were discovered by the old man. They are big, burly, coarse men. Naibhu is frightened, but he soon realizes that they are not going to take him anywhere, that they are in the same situation that he is in. They have no roots, nowhere to go and they are hungry. So Naibhu gives them food. They wolf it down like hungry pack animals. Naibhu wants them to go, to get out, to leave! He doesn't like them but thinks that they might add some information.
   Naibhu has a strong urge to go south. This rocky

barren area doesn't seem right. He wants to go south because every time he turns southward he envisions a great temple in the sky. He believes there are many buildings and riches in the south. Within his vision he clearly sees a mosque-like structure also. He wants to go immediately but instinctively senses incompletion, unfinished business, something that he doesn't want to complete. Perhaps he could learn a language there.

He knows that there is something down there for him; something summoning him, calling him strongly. Again he sees a mosque-like image in space. He has never seen anything like that. He does not know what the domed building is about except that it is oh so beautiful. It is all white and shimmering gold. But what will he do without a language? He cannot speak to these men. He watches them. He sits by the fire trying to understand them. They do things that he does not know anything about. He is afraid to go anywhere that he might be caught. He cannot tell anyone about himself.

He sees that temple every day; every time he stops and looks southward it appears. He sees it looming up, but he does not know how far away it is because it appears in the sky. He doesn't see it on the ground. This temple awakens something in him, a deep longing and knowing that he cannot understand. He wonders if he leaves this area, if he could steal to eat and if he could find a place to hide. He doesn't sleep with the three men down there by the old man. Naibhu runs away every night to go up into the higher rocks to find some peace. He continues stealing and he keeps feeding the group. The caravans are more numerous. The four men are worthless to him. He doesn't want to teach them how to steal because they are greedy. They are not bright men either. He thinks they were thrown off the camel caravans for some reason.

His mind is very confused. It isn't nearly as clear as when he was with the goats or when he was in the cave. He had made some kind of adjustment then, but his life now is impossible. He doesn't want to go any farther northeast because the mountains are getting too steep and the weather is too cold. He knows that there is nothing here but rocks and more rocks. As a boy he had been in a desert, a dry, rocky area where there were things growing. There was nothing growing here. He is tired of climbing always like a goat so he wants to go south. He is afraid to go by himself. He does not know what is there. Possibly what he is seeing is a dream, not real. Perhaps he will get lost going down there. He knows he cannot go back west. In the west, he is hunted. Apprehension keeps him from sleeping. He just keeps moving—moving like a cat. He is searching for something he cannot find. He doesn't really know what he is looking for except some vague security. Every night he recalls the cave and the pretty things. He remembers when he was a little boy and the goats loved him. It was all so simple. Sometimes he would sit and cry and want to be cared for like a child, but there was no one there.

He does not know about gold except that it is bright. He finds out that the caravan men think it is most important by how they treat it and what they do with it. The objects that are left out in the open air for all to see are not as precious as the things encased in something and placed beside them at night; these are worth something! So he starts to steal important boxes. In his frustration, he wants possessions. He starts stealing gold because it gives him the greatest pleasure. He has no use for gold, but its brightness eases his turmoil. The caravan people wear a lot of gold jewelry around their necks. He now has a gold thing to hang around his neck. It is shaped like a crescent moon. He puts it around his neck and looks more like the caravan men. He is as dark as they and he is growing larger. Naibhu would never kill for gold. He only killed to save his life. He does not care about gold at all.

Naibhu is a very sensitive young man. He is haunted with thoughts that he doesn't belong here. But without information he has no choice. It is getting very cold at night. He ranges farther until he finds a deep winding crack between rocks where he sleeps always on the alert for someone who might harm him or steal his food. Early in the morning he returns to the encampment of the old one. The sly three men have their knives drawn waiting for him near the fire. He circles the rocks behind them; he comes up from behind and slits the largest one's throat, alerting the other two. Naibhu has never fought a human in his life and now there are two after him. He runs quickly into the hills. He is much fleeter, sturdier and more at home in the rocks. He knows that he can outsmart them. He is very unhappy having to run for his life again. Now he has killed another man. He hides and he suffers. He knows that the two men are after him and he is running away. He cannot stand killing anymore.

He realizes that he will get no peace at all until he kills the other two men to get them out of the way. He will not run anymore. If he is to live, he has to go after them. He will turn things around and hunt them. He knows he will find them. He decides to kill now and think later.

He starts down from the high hills, around and across the rocks. Now he is vicious, not protective. He is going to kill because he wants to. He knows the men will be together. He has never fought in his life, but this is going to be a fight. He is not going to slit their throats; he could kill one easily, but then he has the other to deal with. He decides he will not kill them in their sleep. They will have to awaken and start after him, or he will not kill them. It is less noble to kill a man in his sleep; he will take them on, awake and alerted. He will not sneak up on them; it will be a hand to hand battle. He is now a cat hunting its prey; he is going to kill premeditatedly.

He finds them down by a big boulder. As usual they are eating some of his hidden food. Disgust overcomes him; they are a bunch of leeches. He knows these two are unaffected by his killing one of them to protect his life. All they want is the gold. Then something overcomes him and he immediately decides to head south, to kill neither of the men; he decides to run south and leave the area.

Chapter Five

    Naibhu starts south away from the two men, his campsite and the life sustaining caravan trail. He hesitates at the camel crossing long enough to find a caravan and steal food for several days. He has no assurance of where he will find food again, so he stashes enough to take him somewhere. He moves along the high desert as morning breaks. This is not an arid place but full of rocks, sand and small scrub brushes. When he approaches an occasional house, he passes. When he sees people, he skirts around them. Naibhu has fleeting images that he has been here before but these pass without understanding. For the first time since he left his beloved goats, he has a sense of relief, expansion, freedom from something. The world seems to open to him. He watches intently for everything new. Up in the rocks there was nowhere to go. Down here he is going somewhere and the direction is clearly marked in his mind. The deepest reasons for his life seem beyond his comprehension. A softness comes to his countenance; his step lengthens and he begins to resemble a playful deer rather than a crouching cat. He is on his way somewhere.

On the fifth day he sees in the distance the place he has been searching for. There are mosques, very colorful ones looming high in the sky. There is a town around the mosques with houses which spread out farther than he has ever seen. There is a very big temple with a round dome that extends a long distance. Naibhu is drawn to that temple as if he has seen it before. The houses are little flat buildings linked together with tiny paths and streets in between. He is fascinated and afraid at the same time. He hesitates about going into the town center; he skirts around the outside of town and watches the people coming and going. The town is like a hub. There is a bustle of traffic from all directions entering and exiting all day long. There are animals too, but some of the animals he does not recognize. Large animals pull carts with goats tied behind them. Humans pull carts laden with food, colorful cloth and odd objects. He can't see enough!

Naibhu stays outside the village but goes in to steal from the gardens at the edges of town. He loves the fresh vegetables; he has not eaten green, growing things since he left the goats and the lovely green valley.

He watches people going and coming—particularly to the mosque and the temple because these fascinate him most. More than anything else he wants to go down to the mosque and the temple. He feels a magnet is drawing him to these places, but his fear keeps him from venturing further than the hillside. People come and go in small family groups. He has a great urge to join them. He becomes very lonesome, and he cries when he watches the people milling about together. He has never known human companionship and now he has a burning urge to be a part of something. He needs people. In spite of his need for people he is too frightened to do anything about it. He is aware that they look different from him. Although he has never seen his face, he does see his skin; it is brown and tan while they are blue and black. They are dark people; they are small and slender while he is big and broad and lighter in color. They wear flowing costumes that look soft, that drape around them as they walk. They carry things on their heads. The women are wrapped so that he cannot see their faces very well. But he knows that they are women. He remembers having seen one woman in the rock houses where he first lived in his cave and he remembers the beautiful lady. There are lots of little children playing in the town. He observes another world beyond what he has experienced in his life. Naibhu is drawn to this. He doesn't know what is going to happen, but he is afraid because his clothes look different from theirs. He wears old, dark and heavy fabric pieced about him; while these people are brightly adorned in light clothing for warm weather.

He knows that this is a time to watch and learn. One day he is down close to the town where he goes fairly early in the morning to watch the people come in from the countryside. He notices a woman coming with a strange cart. She has two small children walking beside her and the cart is drawn by a sleek large eared animal. The animal breaks his rope to the cart; the cart falls down and the animal runs away. Naibhu forgets himself and takes off after it. He has not had much to do with working animals since he left the yaks, but he is very fleet of foot and so he catches the animal. He leads it back without realizing that this is the first time he has ever shown himself to anyone besides the old man and the bandits. He is not frightened. When the woman sees him, she shows alarm at his appearance. He delivers the animal quickly and when he sees her expression of horror, he backs off and disappears. He has never done anything for anyone else before so spontaneously without any thought of himself.

He returns to his hiding place beyond the last house and in some planted trees and he sits there very upset. He is torn by urges that he does not understand. He wanted to help this woman; he wanted to recover her animal. It is easy for him to do anything that requires speed. He is skillful; he runs like a deer. He felt good taking the animal back to her, but when she and the other men around her became frightened, so did he. This odd, raggedy giant coming out of the mountains and around the hills with an animal looked frightening.

He strays into the bushes and sits among some rocks and sobs. The strange feeling that is coming over him is threatening. There is a yearning that he is unacquainted with. What he has known before is the urgency to hide, to run away, to kill if necessary and to steal to live. Now there are strong new urges that he has to cope with. He seems to want to belong to people, to be a part of what is going on in the city. He sees them greet each other as they pass along the road, and he sees that they live and travel in groups. He has no knowledge and no language, so what he senses he does not understand. Yet these yearnings are very deep and create problems for him. There seem to be many things to cope with now and these begin to feel very burdensome.

One night he decides it is time for him to sneak into town. He will go because he is drawn to the town. He goes cautiously through an untraveled path so no one will see him. The path leads straight to the mosque! There are lighted dishes in the mosque making everything glow magnificently. It is more beautiful than anything he has ever seen. He goes up to the door to see better and finds it barricaded. It is so magnificent; he desperately wants to go inside. He peers in through the windows to see the gloriously gleaming gold on the wall with carved things of immense beauty. He vaguely remembers seeing that kind of beauty before.

He stays in this place for some time, hiding in the shadows so that he cannot be seen. It is very late and there is hardly anyone around. He slowly backs away because something is happening to him that he does not understand. He is afraid for his life but that is not new for him; he has always been afraid for his life. At this time he moves away from the village up into some rocky areas. Rocks are home to him—security. He leaves his green bed amongst the trees to run away to the rocks again. Here he stays for a few days.

He eats very little; he is not hungry. There are other things on his mind besides his stomach. He steals some goat cheese that is sitting on a little shelf behind a house. He remembers that when he was a young boy the men with the yaks gave him goat cheese. He knows that he will go back to the temple. He hesitates with the thought that he might be caught, yet the impulse to return is so great. He listens to a gong and a man who chants from the top of a building. This happens a number of times a day, at special times. The chanter seems to be calling people and many people respond, hurrying to the mosque. Naibhu is very curious about what is happening.

One day there is lightening and thunder that rocks the whole area. This village isn't in a valley, it is on a plateau with hills around it. The rainstorm is huge. It blows and the water runs everywhere; people disappear inside—everyone scatters. Naibhu knows that he can safely go to the temple now; there is no one there. The people are taking their animals inside for shelter. This looks like a monsoon! It rains and rains without letting up. Naibhu waits a day. The more it rains the more he has an urge to go to the temple, to go inside and have a look. It is quiet and there is no sign of humans or animals out on the road. He cautiously makes his way up the road that leads directly to the back of the mosque. The mosque is open and empty; it is all his, glorious, shining and full of color. The ceilings are extremely high and made of gold. He touches everything he can reach. He learns by touch, by handling things and feeling them. The "beautiful lady" returns to him and holds his hand. She leads him to see all of the nice things, the magnificent things in all of the side rooms. He feels that he will burst with excitement at the elegance of the place and the warmth of the beautiful lady. He wants to stay close to this; he does not want to return to the wilderness. He doesn't understand what is happening. He leaves and goes out the front door into the pouring rain. He goes down the road to the temple.

The temple is different. It is not as big. At the end sits a golden Buddha. As he approaches the Buddha, he feels that he has come home. He doesn't know where he is and he doesn't care. He is at peace. His self-concern and self-protectiveness are absent and unimportant. The turrets of the mosques had brought him south. He saw these from a great distance as a mirage. But it is the small temple that feels like home.

He slides in a partially opened door and immediately feels swept upward. Contentment is his. He no longer cares what happens. A decision comes to him that he is back where he belongs and will stay there. The "beautiful lady" stays with him for a long, long time. He doesn't know how long he is there because the rain is pouring down outside and no one disturbs him. Naibhu feels a touch on his shoulder and looks up to see a man in a long robe. The priest jumps back when he sees Naibhu, startled by this huge, raggedy man with long, matted hair and beard. Naibhu is kneeling with his hand on the foot of the statue of the sitting Buddha. The man utters something excitedly which Naibhu does not understand causing fear to return. The priest walks away quickly and Naibhu immediately returns to a state of bliss, imagining that he is telling the priest how he feels, that he is home and wants to belong to this place and these people.

The priest returns with others who encircle Naibhu and as they move closely around him, he is frightened again. He tries to talk to them but no words come. Finally, they come up close, quizzically watching him, noticing his large, dirty hand on the Buddha's foot. When he stands up everyone jumps backwards. He is really so very huge, head and shoulders taller and almost twice as wide as they are. Again Naibhu is frightened because of their alarm, but he knows he will not run away. It makes no difference what happens; he will not return to the hills again; he will not kill again or steal again.

A man begins to ask him a lot of questions. Naibhu hears but cannot understand him. The man seems to be trying to find out who he is and where he came from. Naibhu is unable to tell him; he does not know. Naibhu stands very passively and quietly. They lead him down the city streets to a big stone building. There are steps to a lower level leading to a large room with little stone partitioned rooms off of it. They put him in an ugly little room with a barred grate at street level that lets some daylight in. He has never been confined like this. His cave was small, but he had always been able to see the daylight and have space around him. Now his space is gone. There is a space above the walls of his room before the ceiling, slightly above his head. This resembles a stall for animals. He knows he can climb over it easily which comforts him.

They have locked him up; they have incarcerated him, and he was not resisting. Inside the temple he was overcome with feelings which made him unable to resist with force. Ordinarily he might have wrung their necks with little effort. He could have raced out of the temple and disappeared into the hills, but a strong voice inside him said, no! Something has touched him about the village and the temple and its people; his fight is gone. He looked at the people knowing that he still could get away, that he could physically handle all of them or outrun them and be free, yet he could do nothing.

That night he does not sleep well. The bed of stone is not new to him; the walls around him upset him and frustrate him, and so he does not sleep. In the morning they bring him some ugly gray slop in a dish. It smells like mutton or goat, like the food that the yak men ate. He feels sick and hardly eats.

Two young, weak looking men come into his cell.

Naibhu could pick them both up and butt their heads together. Such is just a passing thought. Without ceremony they take off his clothes and then strip him down. He does not care. Clothes are only protection from the cold and it is not cold here. They leave a basin of water for him to wash with. Naibhu just looks at it; he has never washed his body before. He drank from brooks and washed his hands but never his whole big body in a tiny basin. So he leaves it untouched. When the men return, they unceremoniously throw the water at him. What a shock! The water is cold. He is doused with water, head, beard and body. This is the first bath that he can remember.

Chapter Six

These are not unkind people at all. Suddenly Naibhu knows that this is where he is going to learn to talk. As long as he stays here they will have to come and take care of him and talk to him. This idea excites him. His eyes smile. He is stark naked, wet and smiling. He has found his teachers. He gives them the job. They are kind men; they take care of him, and he will learn to speak. He can tolerate to live in the little cell without daylight if he can learn to speak here.

They come to take care of him or give him water or bring food, and they speak words. Immediately, Naibhu repeats clumsily every word. They look at him strangely. He repeats a word rapidly, and when they leave, he goes over the word until he has it right. Now, he does not know what the word means but he is speaking. He is busy and happy all day long with his words and sounds.

Sometimes he will forget one word which upsets him. He talks words all day. Often he thinks that he has a word wrong and that the words did not go together, but they are human sounds and he is making them again, and so he is content.

For many days he wakes up speaking, repeating a word to be sure he knows it. He is like a baby who by laborious attempts, learns to stand before moving. He has to speak words in order to learn to speak a language. These are pure words, unconnected, that do not seem to have a relation to anything. His mouth could not form words easily at first, since for fifteen years he had spoken to no one. He communicated with the goats in non-verbal ways. Certainly, he did not speak to the yak men. Over time he had lost his ability to speak. Now the word is important whether it has any meaning or not. To Naibhu the words carry pure information of his accomplishments even if they come out sounding strange at first.

He misses the birds, the sky, the winds and the fresh smells but he has people. They speak and he listens intently. He can hear them over the tops of the wall, so he is never without the stimulation of language. He forms new sounds and words although his mouth does not seem to know where to go or how to move to imitate sounds like those that he hears. His mouth plays with sounds. When they say a word he watches their mouths and their lips. He watches how they move their faces to speak.

In his imagination he goes back to the temple many times. Once he has seen something he remembers every detail. The experience he had at the temple repeats in his memory so often that he practically lives there when he is not practicing his words. He is studying human beings to understand them. He is not afraid of these people; he knows they are not going to harm him. They bring clothes that never fit him, all too short and too tight but the loose material works. He likes the loose material wrapped around him because in it he looks like his caretakers.

This is a time in Naibhu's life unlike any other time. He is locked in and he hates the porridge, but his work occupies his attention totally. All day and for most of the night he works forming words and making sounds that sound like the other people. His work is not to understand, it is to make words. The men come often to bring the food and water in a basin. Now he knows how to throw water on himself. He almost likes doing this.

He begins to speak words at them. The incoherent ones puzzle them, but they know he is talking. They share his joy. He gestures for them to make new words so that he can learn more. He plays with one or two words all day.

He daydreams about the temple. At times he remembers his life of freedom. There was no joy anymore in being a hunter or hunted, since he had murdered men. Now he is only hunting words. He does not care that he is unable to go anywhere because now something else is happening.

The "beautiful lady" never leaves him. She listens to him when he talks. At times he talks to the walls. He talks to the Buddha, the sweet, serene face that he does not know but yet he knows so deeply.

He dwells inside a building that looks like a stone prison. The helpers wear weapons. He hears someone scream often. There are a lot of strange noises that do not sound like words. He knows people make these noises, but they do not sound human. These noises make him wince; they make him uncomfortable. This is not a prison for criminals but a prison for the insane; the priests think that Naibhu is insane like the others in the prison.

Chapter Seven

Naibhu is still in the prison a year later. He knows that it is spring outside; he was imprisoned in late summer and now he smells spring again. He recalls spring when the hills and mountains were covered in fresh flowers; the birds and new baby animals are so happy in the spring. He would sit for hours watching the young animals, fumbling to learn. He watched the flowers opening and he heard the birds. Life came alive in him as he ran and jumped over the rocks.

Springtime is the time when Naibhu is happiest. The trees and bushes are reborn. He is very depressed this spring that he is not free. The kind of peace and contentment that he has had for a year is now waning. His deep involvement with learning to speak and to learn is no longer there. He knows what words mean enough to converse now. He knows many words, and when he speaks to people, they understand him. He has learned fast. Now his motivation isn't there any more. His mind drifts to his life's other needs. He wants freedom in the hills, where his body can extend itself and can feel, experience and conquer obstacles. He is sitting on the bench in the empty room where he sleeps and lives. His hair and his beard are shorter; the men keep his hair cut short. He is draped in flowing clothes which feel a part of him now. But he is depressed. When he hears those unknown people let out weird noises, he feels sharp pains. He is less and less passive about everything; he is increasingly restless because his mind is no longer focused on speaking. He remembers the long hours that he spent mouthing words until they sounded correct. Now he can talk words and simple ideas with the three men who come to take care of him.

He has a great urge to leave, to go. Now he feels he is being held against his will! For as long as his will was directed to learning to speak he did not feel held against his will. Now things are different and he wants to go back to the mountains and be free. He wants out so he can learn to live outside.

His three caretakers are kind men. When they come to take care of him, they cut his hair and they show him how to wash his beard. They are the only people that have been really kind to him. He is grateful to them for this. He lets them know he is very unhappy by telling them that now that he can speak he does not belong there. They agree with him that he is not like the rest of the prisoners. When Naibhu asks them to let him go, they say they can't. They agree that he is not like the rest of the prisoners and they agree that he does not belong there, that he has done nothing and has never caused a problem, but they insist that they cannot release him. They are not in charge; the decision is not theirs to make. He asks them to talk to the people who make the decisions and convince them that he does not belong there. Every time they come back Naibhu tries to persuade them, but it becomes clear that the decision has been made that he is to remain in prison. He tries to bargain with them. He asks how long he has to stay. There is no specific time. Naibhu says that if they let him out he will work at anything they want; he will pay whatever debt he owes. Every day they talk and every day it is the same answer.

Naibhu becomes despondent. He does not know what he is going to do about it, except the anger keeps growing. He knows how wrong it is for them to keep him here. He becomes violent. He has never been violent except to save his life. He decides that he is leaving. The first time one of these men comes into his cell, he will grab him and make the guard set him free. He will force him to open the big door leading to the street. He sees that door; he imagines the door; it is the only thing keeping him from freedom. He sees himself escaping through that door. There are only a few steps up to the street and the road. He is going out that door. His violence tapers into depression when he thinks of the men's kindness. He tries to convince them to turn the other way while he escapes. They won't do it; they fear they will be punished.

One day he calls one of them into the cell under the pretense of needing something. Naibhu catches the keeper by the neck and forces his way outside the cell taking the keeper with him. He bolts up the stairs to find the door locked. Naibhu commands the keeper to unlock the door and the keeper refuses. He throttles one of the keepers while commanding the other to open the door. Both refuse. Naibhu realizes that he will have to spend his life there only because these men will not open the door. He is certain that the door is the only way out. There are no openings in the building at all besides the iron grating windows that open up to road level. He hears noises in the hallway. He does not know what to do. Both men are not strong enough to put him back in that cell. Never will he go back alive. He will die for his freedom but will not reenter that cell. Naibhu struggles to clear his thoughts. He knows if he goes back to the cell he will not want to live. The time has come for him to leave. The way out is through the locked door where these men stand between him and freedom. He makes a decision. He quickly grabs the second man around the neck in a grip that he cannot loosen. Dragging them with him, he charges the door. He rams their heads on each side of the stone doorway and drops them. Both are killed instantly. He kicks the door open, tearing it off its hinges.

Chapter Eight

It is twilight outside. There are a few people walking but they do not seem to see him. They look his way but they look right through him. He is dressed like everyone else. He moves quietly down the streets, but he runs when no one is watching. When he gets to the edge of town, he runs as fast as his weak legs will take him. He knows that they will be after him soon.

He recognizes an area on the side of the road, so he walks in that direction. He knows he will be hunted and he cannot stay anywhere in the area. He knows how to move at night...and decides to get a long, long way from here. He runs up over the hills southeast again evading the roads. Finally, by daybreak, his feet hurt so he lies down, but he cannot sleep. He remembers the two good men whom he has just killed...how they taught him to speak...how they befriended him and brought him food.

He has not thought about his decision to kill them until now. It seems he is faced constantly with impossible decisions. He tries to rest but is emotionally tormented. These two poor souls were kind to him. He waited a long time in the hallway for another way without killing. Naibhu is so broad that he could just barely clear the doorway. By placing the men's heads under his arms and running for the door, he could kill them both as their heads hit the stone doorway. Now he wishes he had taken his own life and ended the whole thing. This had not happened. The decision to kill his friends came so suddenly; he simply followed the impulse as if it were the only option.

As he walks along the road, he sees a man in a field plowing with an old stick. He is pulled by an animal, a cow or something. The field is very rough with rocks so big that these stop the animal. Naibhu pulls the cow and removes some of the big boulders. The man stares at him nodding his head in thanks as Naibhu moves down the road. He feels better.

He comes across a woman with several children. They are all carrying very heavy things. He takes these from them and carries them lightly down the road. He feels a strong urge to help people in whatever way he can. He has killed two friends. He had loved them in a way that only Naibhu knew how to love.

Several days down the road Naibhu comes to small village. The houses are separate with lean-to barns connected. It is a farming village and the people are farm people. He immediately wants to work here. He wants to serve and be useful and to do physical things. This time he does not pause. He strides into the village where he looks around without hesitation. He steps right up and asks the first people that he sees if he might find some work here. These people have light brown skin. He doesn't look wild now because his hair is cut and his beard is short and he wears clothing similar to theirs. He finds a roadside produce market and asks for work there. He is told that these people are poor and cannot pay for help.

People come from all around to look at him. They ask him where he is from and he says "north." The people do not know what to make of him. They insist that they don't have any work. He insists that he will work for nothing. He just wants to be with people and to help them. This is very strange to the villagers. He walks up a hill thinking about these people. He thinks he can feel at home here. He retraces his steps and goes back down the hill. He looks around and he sees that he can help. He finds some trees and some rocks where he will sleep well. Each day he comes back to the village where he helps people. He finds a community of goats at the top of the hill and decides to live near them. He talks to the goats this time. He remembers how to communicate with goats; they love him immediately.

He tells the people that he knows a lot about growing things and about nature because he has dealt with it all of his life. He likes these simple people. They work with their hands out in the fields and he understands that. There is no temple here; there is no Buddha and there are no gongs. These are just farm people. He sees that they are intrigued by his size and his strength. They do not understand why this big man, who has walked in from nowhere, wants to stay in their little community and work for food only. A man who owns the goats notices Naibhu with them and offers his barn full of goats to Naibhu as a sleeping place.

Here he is, a goat boy again. Sleeping on the hay near his precious goats. The man gives him food which he takes back to the barn to eat with the goats. He can talk; he has work to do; he has people to be with and he is peaceful. Every day he rambles farther to see all of the community, to know what is going on everywhere, to know every farmer and to offer his help.

This is the prettiest little place he has ever seen, all green and lush with rolling hills. Everyone is busy working and there are goats... lots of goats. He hopes he can stay a long time. He is getting acquainted with the people and the farms and all of the animals. He seems to be an overseer for he watches over everything with a tremendous amount of love and caring. He tells every person that he is there to help as though he has unbounded energy and time. He sleeps on the hay, hearing his goats milling around him. He is happy as if he has come home. The fear of being discovered leaves him.

Nothing happens for a while; he just continues there in the farming community. The man who owns the goats lets Naibhu take the goats out into the fields each day and he brings them back at night. When the goats start having kids, he is in his glory because he knows all about birthing little baby goats—how to help them. He picks up the newborns if they are weak; he holds them and cleans them. He feels like a very important and needed man. All the goat farmers want him to come and help during the goating and so he does.

His purpose is now being realized. He is helping people and since he has known and lived with goats from the age of five to the age of eleven, he remembers caring for mama goats and baby goats. He tells the farmers what he learned. He knows more than the best goat farmer even though the goat farmer has been herding goats for his entire lifetime. He knows because the goats themselves told him what to do. He moves from farm to farm to see if everything is fine with the goats. Some farmers only have a few goats, others have many. The days are beautiful, clear and warm and he is busy and happy. The strength that he lost in prison comes back to him even more fully.

Naibhu helps the farmers with the plowing. They call him when something gets stuck or something falls down which they cannot pick up. Then the children come. All of the little boys in the village rush to see him. He teaches them what he knows about the creatures that crawl in the grass, about the flowers and the trees. He is a good teacher because he has learned by experience. He is so happy as he starts to teach and the little boys teach him more words. Now he has words to describe things other than food and survival necessities. He can explain deeper knowing. As he teaches the children about nature and animals, they teach him words about abstract things and feelings.

He is so happy that he works very hard teaching the children in the afternoon after all the animals are taken care of. He eagerly looks forward to the children even when they are sick. He goes to them and he seems to help them. That reminds him that when he was a small boy...which he has almost forgotten...when he was so close to nature and the animals before he had run away to become a robber, he just lived harmoniously with the goats, the birds and the squirrels. If the animals were ill or injured he held them. Most of the animals recovered.

Naibhu's life reminds him of the past but now he seems to have more. He has people; he has food; he has a place to live with the animals and most of all he has children; the people like him. He belongs! This is the first time he has ever belonged to other people or to a place. It is real.

These sweet and simple people are not very imaginative, but they are so comforting to Naibhu. They have not learned very much in all of their years, but they are good people and they like him. They even look to him as their leader. This is new. He never led before. He never had anyone to lead until now. His only opportunity to lead had been with goats. Yes, he was a goat leader, but now he is a leader of people who come to him for all manner of things.

His speech improves. Money is not exchanged for his help; he does not take money; he does not understand money. The villagers provide his food and clothing which is all he needs. They are happy to do this. He never asks for provisions; they are supplied beyond his needs. Slowly he comes to love these small, dark and willowy people who accept him without questioning his prior life. For the first time in his life he is constantly happy.

Every day something new happens. He relishes new demands openly for he has tremendous resources. They share information with him; he is so curious. Many times he understands more than they do. They call on him to fix things when these don't work and he does so quickly. Women, children, men and merchants ask for his opinions about everything.

As a result of his work the crops grow better, the animals produce more, the children flourish and the community improves. He knows that he is responsible for this and for the first time he understands why he is around.

So, Naibhu again is a big and gentle man, one who experiences a great deal of love. He wants nothing else. His life is happy and apparently complete. At the end of each day he is tired for he does many things. He lifts rocks; he tends sick animals and assists them in birthing; he moves and carries animals from place to place and he teaches children. He goes to sleep each night on the barn hay a very happy man, full of purpose, brimming with wonderment at the fact that he is the leader. He dropped out of nowhere and these people have chosen him as a leader.

Occasionally he remembers the experience in the insane prison. He is grateful that he has learned to speak so that he can work with these people. His language is now almost equal to theirs. Occasionally he thinks about the two men who taught him to speak and denied him his freedom for many, many weeks. He remembers that he begged and pleaded with them to turn their backs and let him go free. As hard as he tried to forget about the incident of their murders, he could not totally eliminate it from his memory. He covers these thoughts with this new life, generous with receiving and giving love.

The crops prosper. He knows about weather from the years he has spent unprotected from it. He tells the farmers when to plant, when the rains will come, when to breed the animals and when to harvest. He is amazed by his own skill because he has never farmed, yet he seems to know all about it. They ask him about farming and his answers always work. They are generous with their appreciation.

Physically, this village is a group of ten houses clumped together. The fields are behind the houses and the little dirt road comes right through the center of town. Occasionally travelers come through but there are never very many. He found this village by traveling in a southeastern direction from the city of mosques where he spent a year in the prison.

Chapter Nine

    Naibhu starts to learn the people's customs. He does not know about customs...of how people live and think. He has words but he does not know what people think about. They seem to think different things than he does. On certain days they wear strange clothes and carry ornaments and make music. He is fascinated. He has never seen anything like this. As he begins to feel comfortable with the people, he starts to notice other things about them. At these ceremonies they do not act like themselves. They talk to people who do not exist or that he does not see. There seems to be something formal about these times as if everyone knows what comes next. Some people did different things but it all works together. Naibhu stands dumbfounded on the sidelines when these events take place.

    He does not know the words that they use when

singing together. He likes it when they just make sounds; the "beautiful lady" always comes to be with him when they do that. He wonders if she understands and why she does not tell him. They bring out some funny looking flat wooden bowls with strings from which their fingers draw plaintive sounds. He has heard these sounds once before in the evening around the caravans. He is not too sure about it—the weirdness sends quivers up his spine. It is not like birds, or animals or voices—it is the "other sound" that intrigues him.

They jump around a lot, sometimes alone, sometimes together and sometimes holding on to each other. It is at times smooth and pretty and other times vigorous and exciting. He has jumped around when he is happy but this has some reason. They call it dancing.

Afterwards they cook special things together and eat a lot and laugh. These celebrations generally only last one day although people talk about them afterwards. He feels more comfortable when people are back to normal, after the ritual is over.

After one celebration he asks to hold a bowl instrument. It is given to him to take back to his hay house in the barn. There he sits in the hay strumming the strings and listening to the sounds he makes and finding out how to change sounds. He is like a child with a new toy. He was in tune with bird songs and chatter. Now he is creating music like birds. He tries to sing also but gives up because it is worse than the first time he set his mouth to create words. In a few days he returns one instrument and borrows another. Although the instruments look alike, they feel and sound differently.

He asks people about their ceremonies. Why do they do these things? They tell him they have always done these things since they were children. Their parents celebrated the same way. They ask the gods to help them and thank them for their prior help. Naibhu doesn't fully understand. He has not needed a ceremony, but he is often grateful to the "beautiful lady." Perhaps this is what they mean.

Music becomes so important to him that he tries to sing with them. They encourage him. His voice is very big but once he tames it he likes it. It reminds him of the time he learned to talk. He plays with singing in the same way that he played with words. He mouths the tones and the sounds. He begins toning because it is easier to make more sounds when he does not put in words to make a song out of it.

He tones everything. He walks all over the fields toning. He tones to the animals. Like the perpetual whistler and the hummer, he is a toner. He plays tones up and down his throat and enjoys every moment of it. He wonders why he enjoys this so much and why he cannot stop toning. This is his perpetual ceremony that he performs on rising in the morning and on sleeping at night. The tones feel to him more important than the words. Through toning he begins to bring memories to light. He remembers his boyhood with the goats; he vaguely remembers earlier times trailing behind his father making little boy sounds; he remembers seeing the Buddha.

Suddenly Naibhu becomes dizzy, not quite oriented. He sees himself as a tiny little boy barely walking in a Buddhist temple. The little boy is following a man, his father, who seems to be an official in the temple. He remembers this clearly as if he is still there in the temple. Priests are toning and chanting. They do not sing like the people in the village. The little boy in Naibhu's memory makes little boy noises as he follows his father up to the place where Buddha sits. The father does not restrain the boy from approaching the Buddha though the other people never come close to it. His father is a very big man to Naibhu then. He does not remember anything else of what happened. He comes back to his senses very disoriented.

Chapter Ten

Naibhu stays in his barn where he lives and sleeps for long periods of time because he is reaching and searching for something. He needs to be quiet. Something that he seems to have known before, when he was a little boy, connected with the music...the toning in the temple, comes to him in sounds and pictures haunting his mind.

He continues to teach in the afternoon. He takes the children walking in the fields to show them things he sees but does not understand. But he does know on some other level and as he walks, he moves and so he teaches them.

Now people come from a nearby village to see him. They have questions about some crops that are not doing well. Would he come and look at these? So he ventures out of the village quite a distance and he sees the crops.

He finds worms and caterpillars eating the crop. He stays there for several days while everyone moves into the fields and removes the caterpillars. Then he goes back to his village.

As time goes on people come distances to see him about a sick goat or a problem. He always goes to handle the situation which sometimes takes him far from home. Whenever people ask for his help, he goes without question. This traveling by foot continues for a while and then suddenly Naibhu becomes fearful coming home alone at night. He begins to be afraid all of the time. People are coming to him from very distant places to ask him questions about their livestock and their crops. He imagines that they live close to the city where he might be wanted for murder. He has felt protection in his village, but as he strays from it fear returns and festers inside of him.

He is not very happy. The former happiness that he had found in this little village from being needed and a leader doesn't bring him happiness any more. He spends more time by himself. The people do not change; they remain warm and caring. They are growing concerned about him because he spends more time alone. He doesn't know what is stirring inside of him. Somehow he senses....trying to go back somewhere, where he has left something. He needs to find what he has left. Anything he can remember is not enough and he cannot seem to go back further. He recalls the days as a little child living with the goats and how hungry he was at times. He remembers how every time he got very sad, the goats would come and nestle up to him so he would not feel alone. He remembers being challenged in the wilderness and how these adventures of learning something or figuring something new took him from his sadness and loneliness. He remembers running away from the men and going up to the hills and finding a cave, his first home, how he went down to the houses to steal grains, his fear of stealing and his urge to work there someday when he was full grown. Finding the caravans! The memory of the caravans still brought excitement to him; he revisits his cave full of stolen objects and food. All these things that he had forgotten, he suddenly remembered. The night he first killed...suddenly explosively...without warning. If he is faced with having to kill again, he does not want to live because he has suffered too much. He recalls that night when his cave was discovered and ransacked and how it sent him running again. He remembers finding the old man and hoping that with him he would learn to speak. The meanness and the ugliness of the old man was like other people he had known. He stole food for the old man in hopes to learn to speak; he healed him and was sorely disappointed by his greed and carelessness in bringing in three more mouths to feed. Naibhu is still searching, searching for something.

His days are not happy any more. He knows that these feelings come from him and not from the people. The people are very concerned about him. They want him to move into one of their houses and stay inside but he wants to remain in the barn with his goats. Occasionally he gets flashes of a little boy following his father in a Buddhist temple but these leave quickly and seem foggy and unreal. There is something impending and he can sense it well. He lives with increasing apprehension, joyless in his work, moving through his day like a animated carcass. The feeling of being hunted returns, and he is haunted by memories of the murder of his friends in the city. He has no basis for this fear, but it occupies his attention entirely.

Chapter Eleven

All night he sleeps poorly. The "beautiful lady" is with him constantly. Her radiance lights the barn yard disturbing the goats. Naibhu knows her presence and her kindness well; she sweeps around not touching the ground. But tonight she is different; she has more substance; she is magnetic. He cannot take his eyes away from her—and he does not want to break the spell by talking. He feels energy moving to and from her. She distracts his uneasiness about an impending danger that has been with him for days. Somehow she knows something he only senses and does not know. But he does not want to know either. His nagging awareness keeps him jumping from each night noise. Finally he picks up his borrowed instrument, strumming his own sounds and toning until he sees before him a golden Buddha. Then he falls into a fitful sleep. He awakens soon with a start and jumps to his feet as if ready to run.

The beautiful one holds his hand touching and cooling his flushed face. He wonders if morning will ever come so he can lose himself in work and forget. She indicates that she has a message for him. He is eager to know about it. He listens without hearing, but information comes to him clearly as though she has entered into his thoughts. The message is that he will experience a disruption in his peaceful life that will bring emotional and physical pain, but he is stronger, more knowing and human than ever before and that he will forgive those who harm him. He asks quickly how it will come about and if he will live. The answer finally comes. Yes, he will survive but he will fear for his life. An overwhelming radiance appears around him with the knowing that something so profound will happen to him, something so glorious that it will be with him forever. This will guide his life.

He trusts what has come to him—the turmoil is over. He rests until the sun lightens the sky and he awakens, radiantly. As he has done for many months, he washes at the community well and leads his goats to a nearby field. He eats lightly knowing that he will remember this day as the day of meeting with the grace and security he has been yearning for. He thinks about waiting in the barn until someone comes but decides this is unnecessary. He will present himself boldly to everyone for whatever is to happen. When he reaches the central area of the town, the sun is up in the sky. But instead of the usual scurry to care for animals and to do the chores, there is a congregation of people as though a ceremony is about to happen. He sees four strange men speaking with the people. He goes to the edge of the crowd to hear.

A leader of the men who has come from the large village identifies Naibhu immediately as the one who is insane and who has killed to escape. They show contempt saying they have come to take him back for his crime. Naibhu quickly confirms that he is the man that they are looking for, that he is the man they had imprisoned because he could not speak. He adamantly declares that he was not insane. He tells the people that he understood everything that was going on except their language. He tells his people that after he had learned to speak, he asked his helpers to free him. He pleads with his people to understand that he did not want to kill, that he had not even thought about killing—he didn't intend to kill. All of a sudden something happened to him when he saw the way to freedom. He did not think; he just acted. He tells his people that he has killed four men in his lifetime, two who tried to kill him and the two who held him against his will. He tells them that he really isn't a killer. Naibhu weeps as he tells them how he suffered from each killing knowing that it was wrong and wondering if all men would do the same if this happened to them. Now he has learned to love everyone in this town and he has found a way to help others. He confesses that his life has not been worth the struggle it brought him or the heartache for others until now.

Naibhu confesses everything telling the people his life's story. The more he describes to them the details the less they believe. They do not comprehend that such a small child abandoned in the wilderness could live. Although they had heard about caravans going across the plains, these were too far away to interest them. At best, they thought Naibhu was making up a tale, probably lying.

Naibhu tells them that he is now so happy, that he is not running anymore. He turns to the town people to say, "You are my friends and I will do whatever you want. You have given me a life and a purpose, something I have never had before." Naibhu's story is finished; he quietly awaits a verdict.

The man from the big village exclaims out loud, "He is a liar! This man is an insane killer. He has to be wiped out to protect all people!" Naibhu is in a very passive state. He has had his say and nothing is happening. The townspeople come around him showing confusion. They do not know what to do. He looks at them with love. Neither makes a move to do anything for a while. Finally, he tells them again that they are his people, the only people he has ever known and that he is ready to follow what they decide. He will not go back to the village to be imprisoned, however. He will not do that under any circumstances. He knows that the four men are not big enough to take him back against his will, and he will not voluntarily go back either. He will not spend the rest of his life rotting in that place for the insane.

There is an old dark skinned man from the town that Naibhu does not know very well who shouts out that Naibhu must die. They cannot have a killer and an insane man in the village with the women and children. He shouts that Naibhu has always been strange, weird with the animals and plants. Nobody understands what he does but he changes things. This alone was enough for them to question his sanity and to fear him. The man warns that someday the men will return home from the fields to find a massacre! Naibhu goes into shock. The men become restless, milling among themselves. Voices are still—nothing happens. They move around him stopping then starting again. Tension is high. Naibhu thinks he cannot keep going through this. There is no safe place, no response except running and hiding. He knows he will not repeat his past escape patterns. Without further recourse, Naibhu agrees with the people and the old man saying, "Yes, as long as I live your lives are in danger—danger that sometime I will kill again." He tells them that he did not ever think about killing; he just did it and he might do it again. A few brave men in the crowd exclaim, "No! You would not kill." Naibhu responds that he does not know that he would not kill. If he thinks he has to he believes that he would. He is sure that he would kill if he had to. He asks his people, "Take my life, then I won't kill again." His confession of weakness is final. A wave speeds over the group. They swarm around, preparing to hang him.

Naibhu stands passively, relieved that his nightmare will be over soon. This remote knowing has been with him for weeks. The "beautiful lady" has let him understand its reality. Good! Good! He wants death. He does not care how he dies as long as he dies quickly. The remaining few people come from the houses circling around him. The decision is made to hang him here. There is great excitement—people seem relieved. They tie each of his wrists with a strap which goes up over the top of the two large spread posts where they hang goats after slaughter. Many men pull the straps until his feet are off the ground, not far because he is so heavy. With straps around his ankles, attached to the posts, they spread his legs apart. After stripping off his clothes they beat him across the back and stomach with knotted thongs. The original agony from the weight of his big body stretching his limbs apart is so intolerable that he enters another state. They strike him hard but he feels nothing. He is having difficulty breathing. As his arms stay tied and his body drops his ribs expand and he cannot get air. He is "spread eagle," the position used with slaughtered animals to scrape out the entrails. He had cleaned goats for food many times although he winced each time. Strange, he thinks, that he does not even hurt. Even stranger, that he will die at the hands of others like animals do. He hangs on a goat stretcher, pulled in two directions. He has no pain at all. The people, are around him striking him and cursing him. The little boys are throwing stones; some of the boys spit on him, yet there is no pain. He sees his body but he is somewhere else. He watches the people and their sadness as he remembers that they gave him a life. He has asked them to destroy him so he cannot kill again. He has emotion but there is no physical pain. Again he is aware of the gentleness of the people beneath their act of hostility. He forgives them. All of the pain and the suffering is over for him and there is quiet. He sees it all as he hovers above them. He has left his body.

They tighten the ropes when his body sags. He writhes to feel better. His arms are stretched as far as they can stretch. His legs seem removed from his body. He barely breathes, yet there is no agony on his face now. He feels nothing. He is passively recalling his life, earlier memories than before. He remembers his mother. She left his father. She took him with her when he did not want to go. He belonged with his father. He did not want to leave him, the temple and the beauty—it was his life. From the beginning the trip was miserable for him. He fought with his mother; he protested that he would not go. Each day he told her that he was going back to his father. The caravan people could not hold the willful little boy and had to tie him down. His father did not know he had gone. He did not know for several days. They untied the boy when he was too far to return to his father. He ran away from his mother at the watering place. He knew he could not go with her, to some distant land where she was born. He thought somehow he must get back to his father. When the caravan went on he ran after it, afraid for his life. He really didn't want to go with his mother; she didn't understand him or his father.

As Naibhu hangs he realizes that he had chosen his primitive life from the beginning; that he was never abandoned. He sees that they searched for him for a long time before the caravan went on without him. He did not know that before. Now he sees himself clearly as a little boy who knows that he came into the world to do something that would be impossible if he went with his mother. His drive was undeniably stronger than his ability. He was hungry, too little to run far. He remembers that he had chosen to hide and be left behind. He had chosen everything except to kill! He never consciously chose to kill.

Naibhu is in a high state—the "beautiful lady" is with him with all of her radiant love. He thinks that death is going to be very pleasant. His awareness is not connected to his body. He looks down upon these human creatures with benevolence.

It is getting dark. Naibhu's body is still hanging and it is cold outside. His head is on his chest. He is still alive! His muscles are so stretched that he seems to have lost his shape. The people have gone. He drifts remembering the people. They saved him and loved him. Now they are torn people...tormented by their confusion between love and hate; they are left with a great fear of their own intense emotions.

He hangs there without pain ready to die. He remembers his life with a kind of relief. The suffering and the fear he had experienced is gone. He waits and waits and wonders how long it will be. His worthless life is almost gone; it had never worked. He has spent all of his energies just living. He did not have time for anything else. He just had to survive, to kill, to live and learn to do so; it is good that his life is almost gone. He has never thought of life after life. As far as he knows this is the only one and it is finished. It grows dark and is cold. He has no clothes on. There is still no pain but now he cannot feel his body. He can barely see it...but he cannot feel it. He hopes that death will come soon because he is afraid that sensation will come back. He feels heaviness when he is back in his body. Night comes and he lapses into states of non-memory. He does not remember or see, but he is watching events cross his mind. In a flash, he remembers the men in the insane house, good men. He had loved them. He is glad he cannot see them the way he left them. So many flashes. He remembers his mother, a sweet woman who did not understand. She was always confused. Then his thoughts move to another space. He hears music, chanting and toning so beautiful that they drown the memory of shouting voices. He sees his father moving up the steps to the Buddha and he follows him.

He sees golden lights so intense, he loses the reality of his hanging and flogging. Something that is very emotional is coming. He is aware of all levels of consciousness simultaneously. He feels that he has left the earth, ascending. He has entered a divine place where he is in touch with his soul. His spirit is a very powerful spirit. There is no weakness in that spirit at all. He touches the ultimate reality, the wonder of the universe. It is all so easy now—except it isn't. Naibhu even in his weakened condition does not will to move on. It is not his reluctance to die but rather some other reason not to live. He is not willing to live. He knows he has made contact with his spirit. The spirit is overwhelming and it is demanding! He experiences a level of himself that does not wish to know more. There is no clear reason behind it! Part of him is trying to cross over, not knowing... not knowing how to die...it is like he is in limbo. He has no feeling. He is alert, but there is hardly any emotion; there isn't much life either.

All at once new information comes to him as he is dying—Naibhu knows the destiny he has chosen for this life. Now he knows why he has lived, why he kept struggling and learning in spite of everything. Now he knows...he knows what he especially knew as a tiny boy, that he came into the world to be a spiritual leader of men. He recalls as a little boy following his father and the great visions that came to him. A power was his to carry out this destiny. He now taps into the power again. He felt it before he denied it! He only knows it is the compelling force that makes him always run, not just from danger but from himself. He had been compelled to run away. He knows that if he had gone back with his mother who was not spiritual, he could not pursue his destiny. It was his father's life that was spiritual. With him he was to be trained and to grow as a spiritual leader. This is what has driven him all of his life. To live, to survive, to learn...his destiny! And now he remembers. Suddenly he seems to be surrounded by faint people...people he does not know and there are lots of people gathering; they continue to come from behind bushes and out of nowhere to encircle his hanging form. He is moving back and forth on many consciousness levels.

The people surrounding Naibhu are in purple robes. They are all around him...and he feels at home. He moves to a level so that he can see them more clearly. He thinks that he cannot reach up to that place...he is fighting back and forth between each level of awareness. It is not sure at all where he is going but it is clear...very clear. The destiny Naibhu finds is completely overwhelming. He has been caught up in living, straining and being hyper-alert to protect himself. There has been so little joy, so little meaning in his life, that as he starts to move toward death he enters another phase. All he has known, believed and thought are erased with the brilliance of what is coming. It is absolutely astounding. Things are moving so rapidly now, so fast that he experiences but cannot record in his memory. He only knows that this soul of his, will accept nothing but truth...total truth. The new glimmers of the past are overcome by the light of the future. He sees it all. Spiritual power is coming to this man overpoweringly, to carry out his mission in the world to be a spiritual leader of men! At that instance the power that courses through his body is so overwhelming that it breaks the sinew that hold him in the air. He falls to the ground. When he lands he knows his life is not finished. He knows that he has not died, but he lies there for a long time unable to move.

He is full of energy; his breathing calms; clear thought returns telling him what to do. He knows that he will liberate men who are imprisoned for whatever reason and show them their destiny. He has a purpose; he has a direction...he is stunned. He is alive in a way that he has never experienced before.

He is in terrible pain. His body is torn and beaten. When he was hanging, numb of sensation and pain, he did not want life, now he acutely aches and yet he wants to live. He lay there, sometimes conscious and sometimes unconscious...he is aware that he will live.

He tries to stand but he cannot rise. He is crawling slowly, often collapsing; his muscles are torn. He is so cold...his body shakes and he crawls. He crawls to a thicket of vines. He crawls between the vines and he passes out.

Chapter Twelve

He lies under the tangle of vines for many days before coming to conscious awareness. His first thought is to run again. This time the urge is different; he wouldn't run for his life; he would run in order to fulfill his destiny.

He is aware of thorns in the vines which encase him. This is a big vine patch on the edge of a hill. He has passed it often. He stirs and is very uncomfortable. He aches everywhere in his body. It did not hurt when he was strung out like a goat, but his ache now is intolerable! He is starving. He moves his body slowly, wriggling out of the patch as he had crawled into it. It is dark. He senses that it is early night.

Unprotected from the undergrowth he is chilly. He tries to stand but cannot quite make it. His legs are very wobbly. He sits for a long time and rubs his legs. It hurts his arms to rub his legs. He is depressed. He realizes that he will travel a long, long way. Finally, his legs are firm enough for him to stand, to move gently. He is groaning and grunting from the pain. He stands, a tall and unsteady giant ready to move again. His head is held high. He does not feel strong, but he does feel very elevated and proud. When he starts to move, he walks so gently, pausing before he moves each foot. His hips are so wobbly. He is clutching for something mumbling about needing help when he senses a figure beside him. A man seems to be holding and steadying him. He is a big man, almost as big as Naibhu. He looks again and the image is gone. Naibhu feels him holding his arm saying, "Steady lad." He is a bit confused; his head is not too clear. But he is greatly motivated to get out of there...to move and to start to walk. It is very painful. His thoughts are not very clear and his body is not very stable. He feels the spirit of a man helping him. He is still with him as he walks back and forth. He starts away from the village because he has to walk in order to heal. He walks as if he is learning to walk all over again. To go farther down hill would be too difficult and to go the other way would take him toward town, so he walks back and forth in a short space. He has to walk. Walking clears his mind, helps him to know what to do. The vision of his helper always stays there, holding his hand, his arm, supporting him and telling him, "You'll make it lad, just take your time."

    There is a kind of aggressiveness coming. His body is not very strong and so he cannot move quickly. This recovery is an ordeal that he did not realize was so strenuous, for although he felt very little pain during the hanging, his body has been wracked and it will take time to recover his strength. He is getting more restless now. He feels aggressive. As he starts to remember something, that spirit that he got in touch with...that spirit...that soul...that he is somehow attached to...it was very, very great!

    He is moving back toward the village. He looks up at

the poles where he had been hanging...he looks at them and moves on. He knows where vegetables are kept and stored in a little bin outdoors. He is very hungry. He crosses the road and approaches a special house where there is a little lean-to building. There he finds some clothes, white fabric that men wear around their waists. He takes two of these; one he puts around him and the other he puts inside a straw basket. He does not go into the house. He is not very steady, and he knows he would bang into something and awaken the people. He goes back across the street to the bin that holds the vegetables and some grain before he starts out of town. He takes a knife that he found sticking out of a post. He has not had a knife in a long time. As fast as he can walk, he heads for the main road.

He walks slowly with painful steps and he eats as he walks. This is the first time he has carried possessions. He has vegetables and he has some clothes. He has enough, all that he needs.

He heads for the end of the valley, walking along the rocky ravine, south to a lower level, leaving the road. He stumbles a bit, but he keeps moving down this rocky ravine over boulders. Ordinarily he would have jumped off and run down to the ravine, but now he carefully picks his way, leaning on rocks to stabilize himself. He keeps moving, torn between pain and a feeling of exultation and new purpose. With all of his weaknesses, he stands so tall. He does not find himself running. He feels a defiant attitude of "don't get in my way." It is not the attitude of a killer but more like that of a ruler as though he will make demands on the world from now on. Instead of stealing—he will request what he needs. There is a kind of presence coming. It is new to him and a great surprise. He is not very clear in his orientation of what has happened and where he is going. He does feel stirring although his body moves with hesitance. He has gotten in touch with something that he has never known. It is an exciting time. He is a very important and special soul.

He keeps walking and resting. There is water in the little creek where he bathes the sore wounds on his back. He rests a while and he goes on. He does not dare stop. His body becomes stiff when he stops. His compulsion is to get the soreness out of his body. Eventually he comes out of the rocky ravine. The village he left is up in a high valley...not as high as where he had been before. He has been winding his way down to a flat land.

He has never seen such a vast flat land. It is as flat as water but very green. As he moves he becomes more and more aggressive as if he has something important to do; he is accumulating power and determination as the day and his movement propel him across distances.

The weather gets warmer. As he moves, his body is becoming stronger. He moves for entire days before dropping from exhaustion. At the end of this day, he sees a farming community. He walks directly into the first large barn that he comes to and he knocks on the door. He tells the woman at the door that he is a traveler who would like to sleep in the barn. He does not beg; he asks with a quiet presence that gets results. He has no problem with the farmers. He presents himself as the important man that he is. He wants them to know that he will be sleeping in their barn.

The structure is used as a stable. There are goats inside; he pats their heads. There is dry hay also where he collapses after opening his bundle and changing his clothes. As he lies on the hay, he remains awake full of wonderment. He does not know where he is going. His attitude is that he is going somewhere. He is not running. He knows the people will not come after him. He can see them now. They seem depressed as though they have lost something. It is not very clear. He knows that they will remain in their town. They will not hunt for him; they know that he has escaped and each of them is privately happy that he is alive.

The "beautiful lady" appears to him. She stands beside the hay and holds his hand and talks to him. She says that he had to see his death in order to know about the spirit of his own soul that is so strong and magnificent! She tells him how he had been guided as a little boy by this spirit and how he had lost it during his struggle to live. Now it is returning to his knowing.

He sleeps oh so deeply. The hay feels especially good to his tired, aching body. When he awakens it is still dark, and he has the urge to move and run. He decides not to run away by night; he wants to go by daylight to see everything that he can see. When the light appears, he goes to the farmer to thank him for his bed and returns to the roadway.

His head reaches the sky, for he is a proud man. Proud of what? He is not sure. As he walks along the road, he is aware of his goodness. He is aware of the fact that people look at him. As he passes by people turn their heads to look. He nods to them or makes a gesture and keeps moving forward. He has strange feelings about his thing called "pride." He has had so little experience with it that he wonders about its reality. He does not know where it comes from. Surely he does not have anything to be proud of.

He moves on in the warmth of the sun. There is something nice about his time to travel. The land before him is a continuous run of farms. There are no rocks, no hills, no bare spaces, just farms and many people. He is curious about the two wheeled little carts that he has never seen before. He likes everything in his sight. People seem to be very busy. He remembers and uses the language that he learned, for he feels proud to have learned a language. Every night he asks for a place to sleep saying that he is a traveler, going somewhere. When he runs out of food, he does not steal—he goes up to a farm house and asks to work for food. Generally, they have some heavy work that he can do. He works for a day or so for which they give him food. He thanks them and is on his way again.

Something has happened to Naibhu. He walks so

straightly. His stride is firm and direct. He does not have to worry; he can work to eat. Each night he finds a structure to sleep in, and he knows there are other places wherever his destiny takes him.

Chapter Thirteen

Naibhu walks long, long days. There is nothing else to do; he might as well walk. Only occasionally does he stop to talk to the farmers to ask a question about a crop that he does not recognize. The farms here are small plots of land and the area is more populated. Other than his big size, nobody pays attention to him. He is free to walk. There are many others walking so he blends into the streams of people carrying their loads.

One day Naibhu comes to a village, bigger than any one he has been in since his escape from the prison. There is a temple! It is open so he goes inside. Some of the people are toning! He sits down and he starts to tone with them. He has never toned in a temple since he was a boy in his father's temple. This lovely temple has a gold Buddha at the front. There is incense burning sweetly. He senses the nice people and sits there for a very long time amongst them. People come and go from the temple quietly as Naibhu sits, transfigured. He remembers the temple from his boyhood. It was a different temple from this one. This temple is full of all kinds of things hanging around. It has some pictures and some other figures with the gold Buddha in the middle. What he remembers from his father's temple is a very big Buddha, a huge stone Buddha sitting on an outdoor platform. He would climb big, long stairs to reach the Buddha. It was a very important Buddha. The people did not come too close to that statue, but his father would walk right up to its feet with little Naibhu trotting behind.

In this small temple there is a lot of color, painted things and bright cloth. Overall the temple is very dark inside except for oil lights burning. He sits inside and thinks, absorbing everything. The Buddha has a nice sweet expression on his face. He remembers the only other Buddha he has seen, in the town where he was imprisoned. This time he does not humble himself to Buddha; he sits very straight, very erect and looks at him with loving kindness.

He stays in the temple a very long time, aware of drifting into strange places, hyper-aware, high and yet all there. As Naibhu leaves the temple, he knows he will find many temples wherever he goes. This provides a kind of assurance to him. He has found assurance in a temple with a Buddha. The assurance is a kind of self-assurance. The first Buddha he found in the big village mesmerized him. He was so emotional, so non-rational and so humble that he did not care what happened to him. He had been attracted by something, was stupefied by this attraction and so fixated that he could not leave. Now he does everything with full self-awareness. He comes in, tones, sits with people and when he finishes he leaves on his own, by his own volition.

Now Naibhu continues to move across the landscape. The vegetation gets more dense and the trees more plentiful. Where he had come from the trees were few. He would look down at the trees lining the walk way or the animal cart road with little pathways on the sides for people. In this place there are separate paths for people and for animals; trees line the roadside.

Naibhu becomes relaxed about this journey. There is no turmoil at all. No one is after him. He does not know where he is going, but he can always find a straw bed. There is a lot of food here. There are no problems as there had been when he had to steal from caravans to survive. There was no food up there except what one could dig from the ground or find in a bird's nest. Up there the shrubs and the vegetation were tough to eat. Down here, berries grow alongside the road. The farther he goes the more plentiful is the food. He never steals again. He works for his keep. Sometimes he does little chores and sometimes he does very physical work. People are happy to trade food for labor. Naibhu is moving at a slow and steady pace; he is spending time in each place as he moves; he does not want to rush anymore. Time is needed to find this new man that is emerging in Naibhu. He is growing in strength because he is always moving and working. The "beautiful lady" seems to accompany him. Nothing profound happens. She is always there when the day is over and he rests. He is aware that he needs time to gather momentum toward the destiny that he senses awaiting him.

Chapter Fourteen

He is approaching a city perched on a small hill in the distance. The buildings are tall and bright, colored tan, white and pink. He sees a temple and some turrets. He is amazed by the shapes of the buildings that surround the temples. This must be an important city.

His pace quickens with excitement. He is going right on into the city; he will not slink around as he did the last time. He is quite compelled to get to the city. He's fascinated with the low wall around all of the buildings separating them from the fields. It is early afternoon as he enters through one of the gates...inside — oh, it is dusty. He chokes on the dust. There is no vegetation, nothing green or pretty inside. He walks down the main streets which are the biggest streets he has ever seen. The buildings are jammed together one after another. There are little lanes off the big street that are free of people and that are lined with the buildings. It is very noisy. Everyone is making a racket. People are hollering and shouting; they are even screaming and banging things around. He walks down the middle of the street as if to assert that he belongs here. He looks around without letting anyone know that he has never seen anything like this before. He holds his poise; his head is high and he walks with assurance.

He walks up and down many streets looking into every little alley way as if hunting someone. He is behaving aggressively now like everyone else. He is absolutely and totally fascinated by the city. He keeps moving into the heart of the city where the noises and the smells intensify. He comes to a huge, busy square. There are many vendors with carts and merchandise on the ground. On one end is a market with food, another has clothes and things. People jam into the square.

He goes around to each vendor looking at the merchandise. The clothes, baskets and pretty things interest him most. He notices that the people use something that looks like tin or lead to exchange for things. They use coins here instead of gold. He does not have any coins. He has never had any coins. He has heard of them but has never used them. Everywhere he has lived, barter, not coins was the currency of exchange.

He sees many things he has never seen before. After he surveys the entire market and its goods, he sits in a convenient place to watch people. He had watched the birds and animals to learn about nature, now he has to learn about people.

He sits and watches the people coming and going. He tries to figure out what makes the city so busy. He wonders what the people think about. He is free; he speaks and is learning more about what people find important. There are many vegetables that he has never seen before and grains, too. There are containers, crocks full of wet food, kind of smelly stuff. He looks in each container but does not recognize anything. All of these prepared foods he is not tempted to try.

He is going from place to place. People do not pay much attention to his aimlessness because he speaks their language. The words are similar though they sound a bit different. He asks people about things he does not recognize.

At the end of the square behind the vendors is the temple. He thinks this is great. This city has everything. To him everything is new...the smells are new, people dress differently; they have hats and clothing hanging for sale. He wonders where these kinds of things come from. He knows that women make cloth, but these are ready made clothes. Some cloth is very bright and colorful. He is dressed like the farm people, in old, colorless cloth. These people wear more color. He has his basket but cannot buy anything without currency. He will watch and find out how the people get their coins.

Naibhu goes around to watch the animals. He goes up to one of the men and tells him that he knows a lot about goats; he will take good care of the man's goats. The man does not comprehend so Naibhu moves on. He is pretty aggressive about his need for work. He stays in the animal section because it is familiar, and he knows he could be useful to these people. There is not anything in the market that he can do for coins. He wants coins and he is not going to steal them, so he mills around looking for something, thinking about something he can do to get them.

Finally, he gets work cleaning up manure after the goats. People use the cow manure but not the goat manure. He gets himself a shovel and a pull cart and he cleans up manure. He sees that the manure accumulates and is not being used. This way he has work to do; he can hang around in this city and learn about what goes on here.

Once he gets coins, he does not know how to count them. He knows to give coins in exchange for food. He gathers the manure and deposits it on the far end of town. People tell him where to dump the manure. The work is exhausting because he pulls the manure cart himself. He has no horse; he has to be his own work animal to pull the manure cart.

It is getting dark. The people are leaving the squares. He does not have any place to sleep. He has not seen a barn anywhere in this city. There is a temple, however. He thinks that he will sleep in the temple. The temple is lovely, full of lighted candles. He is tired. He has learned so much and seen so much. He is very sharp in the way he asks for information. He only asks for little bits of information so as not to appear strange. He does not want them to suspect that he does not understand the whole picture of how things work in the city. He asks people for bits of information that he pieces together on his own.

The floor is hard inside the temple. It is not a hay floor. With his little basket of food he curls up and feels very safe and warm with the Buddha nearby. As he lies down to sleep, he gazes up at the Buddha wondering who he is and why the Buddha makes him feel so different?

He is sleeping in a corner where his body fits snugly. It is nice and warm. He falls asleep thinking about the Buddha. Abruptly he is awakened and thrown out of the temple. The temple keepers apparently close the temple at night and toss out the loiterers.

Naibhu is back on the streets. It is dark and he does not like dark streets. Apprehension arises. In the rocks and in the woods, he knows what's out at night. Here he does not know what lurks in the dark.

He roams around with no place to sleep. These buildings all come right into the street, leaving no place to hide. He walks till finally at the edge of the square he spots a bunch of men. He gingerly works his way down there. These are disreputable looking drifters—a bunch of derelicts. There is one crippled man. They are sitting around a little fire. Naibhu steals into the shadows and watches them. They do not seem to have homes either; they seem to have no place to go. They are older men and appear to be full of trouble. They also look hungry so he takes his little basket of food and shares with them. They do not have a basket, so he just goes around and gives each one of them something to eat. He feels compassion for them. They make jokes with him about his giving away food for nothing.

He is tired from a day of moving shit from one side of the city to another. The square looks cleaner than it has ever looked before. Finally, he sits on some rocks; there does not seem to be any place to lie down. He sits there and as it gets later the men curl up on the ground in the market square. Naibhu watches them lying there. He is not happy about lying down amongst them. He takes his knife and puts it underneath him and he goes to sleep.

It is a restless sleep. He has some coins in his belt. How many he does not know. When Naibhu awakens there is a slimy hand underneath him reaching for his knife and his belt. He grabs the culprit at the nape of the neck to have a look at him. What he sees is a miserable and sick looking bastard. After he holds him a while, he knows he has to get out of there. He sits up the rest of the night, watching the slimy men.

He is glad when the sun comes up. He gets some food because he has some coins. He works and begins to ask questions of the passersby. He wanted to know how many coins it took to buy the pretty clothes. He asks where they come from. He is told that the clothes come from the big city down the way, just southeast of here. He wants to know how long it takes to get there. They tell him that by foot it takes a couple of days. He stays around that day, feeling lonely.

He does not stay with the homeless men in the square that night. He goes down the road to the outside of the city where he dumps manure. He sleeps on the banks of a little stream in a thicket of vegetation. It seems to give some protection. He will not be seen sleeping there. He beds down with food, his knife and his coins under him. He sleeps restlessly. He has no one and no place to call his own. He does not like this city very well.

He decides to stay a little longer because he is learning. He is learning about the big city and if he is going to a bigger city, then he has to learn more than he knows right now. So he stays. He has a job. He becomes more attached to his little place out along the stream where he lives at night. Every afternoon he leaves the city to go to the stream and bed down. The air is fresh and the sounds quiet, but Naibhu gets very depressed again. Here he is; he has found a city so far away that nobody is going to chase him, yet he has nothing—no friends and no hay barn. He does not know where he is going. He does not even like the city. In a sense he is running away to hide and sleep on the banks of the stream.

Every day he forgets his depression when he goes back to the city to watch and to see. He sees people moving back and forth with carts and animals. He smells new smells and hears new sounds and asks new questions. That is all he is getting and these no longer make him happy. Each night outside the city he feels like a little boy that runs away and cries. Naibhu is very sad again. The sadness makes his heart very heavy. When he remembers being strung up by the people in his little town and the miracle of how his life was saved, he feels better. Inside the city he does not seem to feel his grandness. He is alone amongst many. He tries to remember the details of what happened and how he miraculously survived. He remembers the soreness and the walking and the determination that he was working his way toward his destiny. Now he does not have any purpose except to learn about a city he does not like. He remembers the man who held his arm and steadied him and called him "lad." He wonders what happened to him and if he was real, for he did not remember seeing him with his eyes. This man was surely his friend.

He has accumulated coins, a bit more than he needs. He brings them back and hides them. He has enough food. He decides to go, to leave the place. He stands up by a tree where he can see the city. The city is not right for him. As he leaves, he skirts the edges of town without going through it. This is the day he decides to go. He does not leave as triumphantly as he came.

Chapter Fifteen

He knows the way to the big city. He has seen the dust from the road for a long distance. It is a busy road. He falls in line walking with the people and the carts.

As he walks, he comes into a cross road between the two cities going north and south. He takes the southern direction. On this road is something different. There are the regular small herds of cattle, people with food and houseware. He sees a big caravan... coming toward him. There are many caravans and Naibhu is surprised by the number of men and animals. They are going north. As they pass him, he turns and follows them a short distance. He remembers the first caravan where he stole food and gold.

He wants to go with one of the caravans to find where they come from and where they go, but he turns back south to a big city. He decides to get some work there so he can join a caravan. They have lots of carts and containers painted bright colors. He does not remember if those others going west were as bright. There are more animals and some camels here. Also, some caravans are going north and some south. The southern trains are smaller; the carts not so loaded. He wonders where they leave their merchandise.

He follows the caravans from close behind. With so many people walking, his curiosity does not attract attention. Finally he comes to the big, big city he has been searching for. He does not want to go inside; he does not like being in a city, so he stays outside in a tree shaded campsite. There are a lot of people out there. He watches as they take the caravan animals into a station or a stockade.

The next day he goes to the stockade to be around the animals. There he finds a bunch of men where he asks for a job. They inquire if he knows how to handle animals. He tells them that he can both drive the animals and take care of them. He does not tell them that he knows nothing about camels. They want to know where he learned about camels. He says he has worked all over. They hire him because he is so very big, and they think he will work hard.

He has never gotten a job taking care of the animals so easily. So he stays there and he feeds the working animals that are separated from the carts when the men take the carts into storage.

The stockade is right on the edge of town. As he cares for the animals, he keeps an eye on the men who work and hang around the animals. They do not look trustworthy. He decides that the next time one of the caravans comes into the city, he will follow and find out where it goes. One does not come for several days although he is always watching.

He sleeps farther outside of town than the stockade. A whole group of people live out there. Some are migrant workers who move around, others are families who do not have homes. They do not seem to be derelicts. These are all people who work and live there. They have a few possessions to cook with. There are small outdoor markets where people buy their food. Naibhu is paid with coins, so he buys food for himself and lives as comfortably as usual. He enjoys knowing that people like himself are near him.

He is not happy waiting; his work is routine. One day he sees a big caravan approaching. He leaves his animals and takes off following behind it. He goes into the huge city. The caravan keeps moving until it comes to a big building. Down one side is an alley to the back where the caravan disappears. Naibhu follows to the back where there is a closed area with a big wall around it. This is where the men bring the animals out and take them back down to Naibhu's stockyard. He understands the city is no place for animals, but the caravans are unpacked and the merchandise is being taken in and out of the building. Apparently this is where caravans begin their journeys. Now he wants to work with a caravan and go where it goes. He is motivated again. Naibhu has problems with motivation; he is either way up or way down.

Naibhu is filled with hope and expectation that something important will happen when he reaches the city. He has been moving quickly away from the memories of the people and places of his past. They did not know him then and do not know him now. He is able to speak and find a job when he needs one. His capabilities keep him independent; he needs no one's help or kindness in order to survive. But his feelings of independence and pride are always mixed with feelings of purposelessness when he is out in the world alone. There is nothing driving him; he is drifting aimlessly; he does not know where to go. Each day he is less and less satisfied. He spends more of his spare time alone where he lives in the outskirts of the city in depression and bewilderment. He occasionally watches for a caravan so he can dream. Now he is unmotivated to pursue even that.

He is so fatigued, that his mind wanders, rarely focusing on anything he can hang onto. His thoughts drift to the "beautiful lady" who holds his hand and comforts him well but never talks to him or leads him out of chaos. The powerful energy, which gives him intense experiences in his life and which sustains him, is absent now. He has little energy, no motivation and great restlessness. He is aware that his "will" leaves him when he has nothing to struggle against. He has lived by his "will." He is now struggling to learn a new personal lesson.

He remembers that since the hanging, he has been almost emotionless, experiencing only depression when he stays too long in one place. He has not felt the emotions of love or hatred toward anything; he has not had to figure out or change anything. It does not seem all right for things to be neutral. He knows he does not want to keep wandering. This running away is a running away from himself and not others. At times he seems to be in touch with his deepest level, the soul, that he found that night on the goat stretcher. That soul is now screaming for release from his aimlessness. He cannot somehow get hold of that higher power that broke the straps that night and saved his life. He is wondering why he is spared when he cannot even remember the destiny that he found. His life seems a worthless struggle. When he can stand it no more, he purposely seeks the lady. She has a very soft energy that brings tears to Naibhu.

One night the "beautiful lady" returns. This time she is animated; she is ready to tell him something. He is so exhausted that he is willing to listen. This is what she teaches him, "You have lived by your will and the emotions connected to that will. The circumstances connected to your life directed all of your energy and all of your power, but it has been directed wrongly. All of your energy has been directed by your "will" into being a human, a physical person and not into being a divine spirit. Some of the power of your soul gets lost in the will to live. Your body lives and your soul suffers." The power of Naibhu's "will" is so extraordinary that it saved his life but lost its focus and created a pressure, a pressure attached to a physical life. Now he must discover a higher "will" which will redirect his life's motivation.

Naibhu is not too sure of these messages except that they affect his feelings deeply. The pressure and the depression lessen with the lady's words. A little lightness occurs as though there is a free energy not commanded by his strong stubborn "will." Perhaps what the lady told him is correct.

The following day he moves into the trees to contemplate the message of the "beautiful lady." He remembers something that brings him to a realization. The course of his life was set in his learned behavior as a young child when to pursue his destiny required that he survive. To live meant to direct his spiritual energy into a will to survive. To this end his direction was clear. In his struggle to exist, his spiritual direction was sidetracked. Naibhu's power was never lost; it was no longer spiritual. His power was stimulated and used to maintain life under acute hardships—giving this power an identity that moved on its own often losing touch with its source. If he had stayed with his father perhaps he could have gradually gained the insights and capacities to become a high spiritual leader—his soul's chosen destiny. But instead his demands were sheer willpower to exist. To continue was almost beyond human capabilities. In misusing his great spiritual power, he thought he could live and that somehow he could return to his original state and awareness of center. But this no longer seems true. He loses sight of his destiny in an attempt to maintain life.

The "beautiful lady" has led him to understand that his "will" directs his energy. When his "will" is strong so is the available energy strong, but the direction of the "will" determines its usefulness. The "will" locks or unlocks the soul's work. He recognizes that somehow he needs to disassociate his willpower from his body and physical needs and redirect it to its proper place—his spirit. He believes that his "will" has served him well in the past; it kept his course straight, made him persevere, kept him from deviousness and dishonesty. But his "will" also keeps him bound, non-creative, non-explorative, merely existing. As he does not stray from his path neither does he reach his destiny. He is driven, not enough to get totally lost—but neither enough to be found. His course has been clear but misdirected. Now he has another task. He has to not only return his spiritual power to its proper place but he has to accept a spiritual strength that is overwhelming to a mortal soul that has not experienced this intensity. And his job is to learn that this power can be and must be manifested in the flesh as well as the soul. Naibhu is becoming spiritually awakened which will serve him and guide him on new paths.

Chapter Sixteen

For the first time in Naibhu's life he does not feel insecure. He seems to have left the first part of his life behind. He does not sense that anyone is following him for his murders. He is not satisfied with his work but it keeps him fed. He can speak and there are people around. In this kind of "drifter's" village, the workers just live outside. There are no structures; they just live and sleep out under the trees. He has all these things and yet he is still terribly sad. In fact, he is lower than he has ever been.

He looks out over the area and he sees a caravan coming. He remembers the beautiful things that the caravans carry. He recalls the carved face of the old man that brought him so much joy and the golden neck decorations that the three men tried to steal from him. Since he left that cave, he has had nothing beautiful of his own.

He remembers the temple...the temple in the first city was so magnificent. He knows that humans create the beautiful things with their hands. He looks at his hands and these are sensitive hands made tough with years of labor. Naibhu has the sensitivity of someone who could make these things, and he feels very moved by man-made works of beauty. But Naibhu has only lived in barns. He remembers as a child following his father to the big Buddha. He hears the music. Now he is with a lot of people, but somehow they are not like him. A very gentle and sensitive part of Naibhu is reawakening. This reawakening makes work with the animals very difficult. In fact, he does not want to take care of the animals any more. So he doesn't—he just sits.

He sits and his thoughts drift until he visualizes a great huge temple, color and music. He will move inside the temple knowing that this is where he belongs. He feels quite at home so he just stays in those spaces. He does not seem to care about anything. He does not go to his work. People are around him but he does not communicate with them. He can talk but he is not interested in talking.

Men come after Naibhu to find out why he does not come to work. He does not know why he will not go to work, but he cannot go any more to care for the animals. The head leader of one of the caravans comes to find out what is happening; why aren't his animals being taken care of? He is angry at Naibhu. But Naibhu is not going back to those animals. He has gotten in touch with something else that he needs more. He does not need to be around rough men in the stockyards. The leader of the men is very violent as he orders him back to work. When Naibhu flatly refuses, the caravan leader knocks him down. Naibhu sits there not caring at all. The simple and kind people that he lives with gather around him. They scream for him to fight. The caravan leader is a big man and a bully. This is how he has led men all of his life; this is what he knows. Naibhu does not care. His anger is internalized in depression believing his life is not worth very much. He has killed for his life, has run for his life. Now he sits there on the ground with a big bully standing over him. The people are screaming for him to fight, but he will not fight. He is bleeding badly from the head but has no motivation to do anything but just sit there.

Naibhu has been in a strange state for days, a golden space without details. Now he hears the voice of his higher self yelling, "Take command! Take command!" It repeats again. Naibhu stands up very big, very tall and very strong. The man comes at him viciously with only his fists; he does not have any knives or weapons. As he comes after him, Naibhu parries his fists, picks him up and holds him over his head. He moves swiftly to a big rock with an urge to bash the man against it, and the same voice comes to him saying, "You are in command." Naibhu lays the man down gently. He tells him to go back from where he came, that he is not a leader of men but a weakling. The man creeps away as Naibhu stands there knowing that he has taken command.

The people rush around him to pat him on the back. He silently leaves the scene to be alone. Something has happened to him that he does not understand. When he took command, he realized the strength of two men his size. Instead of using this to kill a man, he had put him down gently and told him to go back from whence he came and to mend his ways.

He is alone now, wondering a lot. For a while he visits places of color and beauty in his mind. He hears music and all is beautiful. He is told often to take command; of what, he does not know. He thinks the charge is to take command of himself. He sees gold a lot. The people keep looking for him, calling out his name. The more they search for him the more he tries to hide. He wants to be alone.

The people bring him food. They act strangely and seem to want something from him. He sits in a woodsy area away from his campsite. The people come to inquire but do not come too close to him. Some people bow down to him which is even stranger, making him anxious.

Naibhu still does not feel motivated to do anything. He is not out of his body, just caught up in another awareness. None of the other things have any importance. He does not care whether he eats. It seems terribly unimportant. He does not care whether he sleeps. He just sits in a daze. He sees the people come around to bring food, but no one bothers him.

He continuously imagines beautiful places as though his soul is searching for something. Naibhu's boldness is softened; he is quiet and he is gentle. He has things on his mind. He speaks very softly and he moves more lightly. He has spiritual thoughts. This is new for him. Outside of early childhood experiences in the temple and the experience with the Buddha he has not had spiritual experiences. None at all. Whatever is happening seems to put him at ease. He does not hear any music or see temples, but he stays within a golden light.

Chapter Seventeen

Naibhu is sitting on a large rock some distance from the encampment. Rocks have always comforted him. He has the feeling of passivity. The very strong "will" which had directed his life, keeping him alive, seems to have waned. That "will" seems to be very weak right now. He has moved away to be separate from the people. to be quiet, to understand more deeply the changes that he was experiencing. He has insights that bring so many tears, and then these insights seem almost unreal. As he sits on the rock there are all kinds of strange feelings of hanging on. And yet there is no urge to go back to animal keeping. His head is a little fuzzy, but sitting on the rock grounds him in ordinary sensation.

Naibhu's constant companion is the "lady" who tells him what is happening, "You are coming into your power." He asks her about the power as he remembers the incident with the caravan leader. He remembers how amazed he was at that power; he knew he was strong but not that strong! He asks how he can use that power when he does not need it. She tells him that it is a different kind of power.

Naibhu continues sitting on the rock, contemplating a different kind of power. First he thinks he does not know anything about anything, then he snaps into another kind of reality with the thoughts that this kind of dreaming is unusual. He gets angry, declaring that he does not want it. He is not good for anything in this kind of situation, just sitting there on a rock talking to a lady that only comes once in a while. He declares that he is not going to participate. He sits resolutely and defiantly saying, "No, I will not participate. I am not going to do it." In fact, he tries to get up to go back to the people and his camp saying, "The hell with this," but he cannot stand. His legs do not hold him. He falls crumpled to the ground. His anger rises; he gets to his knees and begins to crawl, but he still cannot move. He becomes frustrated quickly. He will not tolerate it; he has no use for it. Whatever has happened, he wants it gone.

He remembers the "beautiful lady" was with him just before he was strung up like a goat to die. This time he does not want her to comfort him. He is very unhappy. The last time she said she would care for things, he trusted her. He wants her to go away now. He is very confused.

He hears some people coming. As they approach he hollers for them to take him away. He had not wanted their help, but now he wants them very badly. He keeps calling and they keep coming. They come right toward him walking all around him, but they do not see him. They think they heard him scream for them, but as they approach they hear nothing and see nothing so they go away.

The "lady" returns. He is in shock now and wants to know what has happened to him. Why hadn't the people seen him or heard his cries for help? She replies to

Naibhu that he is coming into his power. He is lying on the ground weak as a kitten, and she says that he is coming into his power. He is lying on the ground confused with nothing to relate the experience to. What is happening is that he has been a man who has been very sharp and knowing. He hears everything; he sees everything; he senses everything; he is aware of everything, and now he is not aware of anything. He has nothing to work with except these strange things that are happening.

Back comes his "will." He says he is not going to participate. Not at all! He does not know what he is going to do because he cannot seem to walk anywhere. Nobody can see him, but he still has a choice. And the choice is no!

He is very stubborn. He has no recourse. The answer continues to be no! He will just bloody well lie here and stay here until something happens. Something has put the stops on him. Wherever he has been going; he is not going to go! He is going to stop! Stop still! So, he will remain right there and be mad. He thinks "I will not be led. I do not understand what is going on and I am not going." At that stage, it makes no difference to him that he cannot crawl. He cannot walk or crawl; he can holler but nobody can see him. He is really handicapped. He does not want to see the lady either. All she does is get him into trouble. So he has got control now. He will just lie there and be defiant, totally defiant. What is going to happen to him does not seem to make a bit of difference. He has turned it off. His defiance fortifies his exclamation that he will not participate with the power.

Naibhu experienced that same stubbornness as a tiny little boy when he ran away from his mother. It did not seem to make any difference what would happen in his life when he ran away. He wept because he had made the choice to do it...to run away. Stubbornness had saved his life also. It was such a strong part of him that there was not much he could do about it. His "will" could not be broken even by him.

Strangely, his "will" has dwindled now and he is passive. When the power overcomes him, back bounces his "will" to insure that he will deny that power. Even if he does not move from the spot and never stands again, he will not participate with his spiritual power.

He is lying quietly now, caught by his "will." It is his "will" and he knows all about it—he has lived with overwhelming "will." He is remembering coming to this city, the city he has been looking for, where he could find his work and he could live and get some coins. All this had happened as well as some other things. He experienced images of beauty which lived in his head because he could not find it anywhere else. He saw the marvelous temples and heard beautiful music. He quit caring for animals and stole away from the people who were rough and noisy. Then he got lost somewhere. That big man came and roughed him up enough to bring him back a little bit. He wonders as he lies on the ground why he let the man pummel him until he bled. He wonders.

For a while he moves to rational thought of how he got where he is right now. He remembers everything now; it is so real that he is caught up in it. That woman is not with him any more. He contemplates what he is going to do. Nothing much comes up but he thinks something will. Some direction will come to him because it always has. He remembers when he was so frustrated because he had killed a man. He did not know where to go at the time, but the golden city with the temples arose as a vision from the south and he followed it for days until he found it. He trusts that he will see another image to move toward. He waits there knowing that something will happen; it always does.

He is glad that the woman is not with him. She creates more problems. Every time something happens to him she gets in the way. She comes to him so sweet and helpful, and then he always gets into difficulty. It is good he does not see her anymore. She does not make sense anyway, not a bit of sense. Particularly when she tells him about what is happening to him—that power stuff.

He is not going to participate with it; he will just lie there a while and see what happens. He is in control now. He wants to know. He is not going to participate until he knows about the whole thing. He will not be led. He is lying on the ground with few choices because he cannot get up and leave. He swears he will not move until he gets cooperation, an explanation.

All at once he is drifting up to a beautiful place. Since his "will" is watching his body, he can go to a higher point of consciousness and take a look. He allows himself to hear beautiful music. He moves into a golden tinted cloud and he keeps going till he finds a beautiful temple. He walks in and starts toward the front when the next thing he knows he is on the floor. He lies there looking down at himself lying below in the rocks. The two situations are similar, but in one place he looks down at himself lying in the rocks and in the other he looks down at himself lying in a beautiful place filled with music. There are no figures inside, no statues of Buddha; it is just a gorgeous colored temple with great high vaulted ceilings and domes. Then he becomes aware that he has turned golden. He feels bigger than life. He is floating and standing simultaneously, all golden. There is total harmony. He enjoys it for the longest time, looking about, seeing all of the beauty and hearing music, hoping that it will never change. This is a place that he likes; it is his new home. If Naibhu is able to accept this level of his being that is so very spiritual and so very lofty and pure, he can move back and forth in his consciousness with ease, knowing the world in its ultimate greatness, being at ease in this knowing that this is his true nature as it is also that of all humans. His problem is still to bring this knowing to the human level where it can be manifested. His invisibility exhibits his power. But as long as he can separate it—a vision from his real body—he can lie there, look around and enjoy this trip where he can tolerate his divine power. Invisibility is not the full manifestation of the light of God. That is to come to him later.

He is coming back down now into a full physical reality of lying in the rocks. He is aware that his body has participated in the golden light by the tingling, glowing and feeling so light and powerful. It seemed all right to go up there and look around at all that beauty. It was kind of unreal but oh so pretty. It is like a game that he remembers with pleasure. He feels at home up there in his temple. It is gorgeous and he intends to continue playing that game.

Chapter Eighteen

    Naibhu is ready to go down and be with the people. He tries to stand but has difficulty. He is shaky in his bandied legs. He starts down the hill, glad that the experience is over with. Whatever it is, he does not want any more of it! He had come through it he hoped. He is going down very gingerly over the rocks and yet with a great urge to now be with people. He had left them in the beginning to find quiet. Now he is through being quiet. He wants to be with the humans even to hear their bickering and shouting. He keeps walking and walking, stopping occasionally to wonder if he should go back with the people. They had come up to try to find him, and then they couldn't when he was right there beside them. Would he need to explain? He wonders what is going to happen when they see him or if they will see him. He becomes anxious, yet he seems drawn toward the encampment of transient people. They live just under the trees and work in the city. They are nomads, a motley crew. He is not much different and so he needs them. His steps are very slow. He vacillates about going back to them. He keeps walking crookedly down the hill. His legs ache. He sits down to think further about going back to the people. But where would he go if he does not go back? He is afraid of something. Naibhu is moving toward manifesting his profound spiritual power that will cause him to transcend the realities of matter and the senses. This is inevitably shocking as it totally changes one's identity.

Naibhu continues descending very quietly, his head held very high. He seems somewhat in another place but is walking with ease. He is coming down to be with his people. These are people who have been harsh and rough at times so he had felt somewhat separate from them. As he comes close he is glowing. He does not know he is so radiant. As he moves down he hesitates among children who are running and playing and are very, very loud, jumping around like children do. They see him and they stop their jumping and they come close to him. They come behind and follow him as he comes into the encampment. Near one little camp two big men are fighting. He moves in as if to stop them, yet when he comes near they stop. They stop their fighting then they back away from him; he knows them well. And he moves on. As he comes to another camp he sees a mother trying to comfort a child. He moves close and the child stops crying. The mother smiles and reaches out to touch him and he moves on. He finds a dog with its foot caught in a fallen tree. He moves toward the dog intending to free it. The dog is crying and yelping and as he reaches out to move the dog's leg, the dog is free. Naibhu frees the dog without touching its leg, and the dog limps away. He comes to a stream and sits down to drink, but there is no water in the stream, only rocks. He reaches out his hand and water flows. He comes to a little village of encamped people. He walks amongst them and talks with them. He appears to be in some kind of dream state. He stops to touch an old man...an old man with a cane reaches out to him with pleading eyes. He touches his hand and moves on. Naibhu looks as though he does not know what is happening. He speaks to people very tenderly. He makes his way through the camp, speaking to one and quieting another. The little children are hanging onto his legs. He tousles their hair and lets them cling.

He has now gone through the whole camp. He sits down and the little ones come around him on a small flat area. His face looks different. He glows. He radiates love and sends it everywhere...especially to those little children with their eager faces. They have their hands on his broad shoulders; the youngest ones crawl into his lap. With his big arms, he could hold so many. People from the encampment in the ravine follow to see what is happening to their children. He looks like some apparition...nothing quite like the way he usually looked. He sits, smiles and chuckles with the babies. The smaller children hand him a little tiny baby for him to hold. All was hushed—they are all quiet.

It grows dusk and the shadows come from the trees. The little ones are tired. Some of them go to sleep. He gets up and he starts back toward the camp to take them to where they belong. He knows where each one lives. He walks back quietly with children hanging on to his fingers.

He experiences a joy that causes tears to run down his face. He remembers the goats when he was a boy living in the hills. Now he has little children to care for. He does not seem to know what he is going to do with the little children. He takes each child where it belongs and leaves him quiet and happy. When he had delivered the last one, he chooses not to go where he ordinarily sleeps and lives. He goes back up the hill to the rocks, so he can see the sky. He sits down. He is not very clear about what has happened to him there. But he is drawn to it again.

There is a quiet assuredness about him. He sits there and recalls what has just happened in the camp. He has moved amongst the people—just moved. The little children followed him. He knew he had to do it. He comforted people as he had cared for the animals. It seems like kind of a dream that he moves through. He finds water in a dry stream bed. Now he sits on a rock, trying to make some reason out of what happened. It is not reasonable. He had thought that he had no purpose. Yet, he returned to his village with a distinct purpose to minister to his people. Now he is back on his rock, trying to figure everything out. All he knows is that something has happened. He hears singing. He reaches up to the singing to find a chorus. And he is drawn right to the very big chorus singing Hallelujah, Hallelujah! In his imagery he has shed his flowing white garment. He is in purple. His whole being is going up, up to his special temple...beautiful, beautiful temple. A very big scroll is unrolled. It has some words on it that he does not understand because he cannot read. The scroll covers the whole front of the temple. Yet, without reading he knows what is written on the scroll. It says, "You have come into the world to be a spiritual leader of mankind and your time is now." He falls on his face and weeps. He says he did not know anything about being a leader of mankind. He knows only about animals and nature. He does not know mankind. The chorus starts to sing and tells him he will be taught. When he is ready, he will be taught.

The "beautiful lady" is there to dry his eyes and to tell him that his training has already started. He will be taught every day, that he must go quietly away from the people, into the rocky hills, where he will be taught. He pleads with her and tells her he is an ignorant man. She asks him if he is ready to learn. He remembers all the things he had to learn in order to live, to eat and to take care of himself—how he watched the birds and the animals and he had learned. He learned well! He found it a joy to learn and he trusted. But what was he going to learn? He did not know. He thought he knew enough about survival. He did not know too much about people or was he going to learn about people? He remembers he has not trusted people for a long time. And now...now he is supposed to lead people. He does not know where he is going to lead them. The "beautiful one" says she will never leave him again. He will never be alone. He will always have someone to talk to when he is afraid.

He sits on a rock. He feels its hardness. He knows he is here, yet there is somehow some of the beauty from up there down here also. He wants the light. He hears the animals and the birds. He remembers the screams of the insane men. He wonders what happened to the villagers. He sits wide awake wondering, to keep his thoughts from his future. He cannot sleep; he sits all night wondering. She is with him all night and he talks to her while reminiscing. He remembers learning to speak and the men who gave him words. It was like a dream. He puckers his mouth as he did when he first tried to sound the words. He remembers how he killed these men when they refused his freedom. He asks the "lady" if he will ever kill again. She does not answer him except to say, "You shall learn." He remembers these men with great love, these kind and gentle men who fed him, who threw water on him, found clothes for him and who lived with him. He had not believed killing them would be such a burden for him.

The music is coming back. It is a deep midnight blue. He hears the music, but he is surprised because he feels the rock also. He has never heard music as beautiful as this. Then she tells him to sleep. He will be watched over from above. He will be guided through uncharted waters.

Chapter Nineteen

He has not eaten for a long time. He has been sitting on that rock for several days. He is not going back to the little village, to the encampment of the people. He is so depressed that he does not want to return. The weather is changing rapidly with heavy, distant thunder. He does not give a damn. He is stubborn because if he cannot get up and go with the caravan he does not care about going anywhere. He is going to sit there in the rain.

He tells the lady to go away because it is going to rain and he is thinking that is a good way to get rid of her. She does not go. She is smiling at him. He does not seem to be able to get rid of her. He does not know that he is in between, on a hiatus. He is neither—nor. He does not know what is next and he cannot go back to where he was. She gets tired of waiting for him so she sits down on the rock beside him, patiently waiting. He is startled as if alerted by something. Something is going to happen. His ears are attentive. He is apprehensive. He is now even afraid of the dark as though there is something out there. He thinks something is out there. He thinks something is going to come up on him without his knowing so he is alerted.

He straightens up all ears and eyes. He even wants the lady to get behind him so he can protect her. There is definitely something out there. He does not know if he is able to get up from the rock to ward off whatever comes. He has a feeling it is something that he does not know about, something weird. This is pretty new and strange for Naibhu. He is ready to dare anything out there to come out where he can see it. He does not want to stay in this anxious state. He thinks that something is lurking in the darkness. He is ready; the "beautiful lady" is behind him. He does not want her to get hurt.

When the thing comes out from the darkness, he gets a first look at the monster he has created. It is a tiny brand new baby goat! A little, tiny, bitsy baby goat all fresh and new. It comes up to him as quickly as it can move on its wobbling legs. He picks it up and he holds it. It is cold, afraid and it is lost. He holds it very warmly and very gently pulls his cloak over the top of it. It nestles down. It is a brand new little baby. He feels his very big love for this precious new animal. He thinks it has wandered away from its mother. Down where the people are there are some goats providing milk. He believes the baby goat has come to him for a special reason too. He suddenly remembers the days when he was a boy living with the baby goats, especially the newborns. He remembers the sweetness of the pasture, the flowers and how those little goats would come to him to be loved and held. He thinks he has not had anything new and loving to take care of for a long time, not since he was strung up and nearly killed. He has not had any yearning for such love either, now this little baby comes and reminds him.

Now he has a little young, living and growing thing

and he does not want to give it up. He wants to keep it. His depression is gone. But this little baby is hungry. He remembers teaching little baby goats how to nurse because some of them do not know how. He would stick his finger down their throat till they started to suck his finger, then he would place them with their mommy. He gets up without thinking because this baby is hungry. He starts down to find the baby's mama. He has a strange feeling that he is not very strong. His steps are very awkward, particularly with this little goat in his arms. The little goat has Naibhu's finger in its mouth. This will keep it happy until it finds its mother.

Halfway down the track to the encampment he finds that the momma is dead. He thinks he might find another momma to take care of this little one because it is just a new born baby. He discovers another momma goat but soon finds that she will not accept the little baby. She will not let him nurse. So now he is stuck with a baby goat that is hungry.

He visits a family who owns goats and buys goat milk to feed to the little one. He loves the little creature. He has a possession, this little living thing. He does not know who owned the mother. He gets the milk and a little dish without remembering that baby goats do not know how to drink milk. He tears off a piece of his cloak and dips it into the milk. The he wraps it around his finger and sticks it in the goat's mouth. It works! That is how he will feed his little goat. He sops the milk up in the cloth, rolls it around his finger and sticks it in the mouth of the goat. Now he has responsibilities. But he is not depressed any more. He has a little one to take care of and the best part is that it has come to him. He has taken care of a lot of animals, but this little one had no one else but Naibhu.

Something is happening to him. He is not thinking about goats he is thinking about people. The goat has stirred this up within him, and he finds himself drifting upward while still holding this precious bundle. He goes to the temple again...the temple he had found a number of days ago. There are a bunch of people there. There is a big table kind of in a round semi-circle. A radiant man is there with a group of followers around him. He is teaching them about love. Naibhu is not going to go inside; he is just peeking in to get some information about his love feelings, almost to find out if it is all right to feel like this. In his imagination he still has the goat with him. He is clutching it with deep love. The goat is bonded to him—he is its mother and protector. He does not want to let go of him even to go back to his temple. Naibhu sees himself at the back door of his dream temple, like his first temple experience in the town where he was imprisoned. He is so uncomfortable that he cannot go through the front door, so he will stay peeking in the back door. The leader priest is so radiant that he blinds Naibhu. Is this God himself? He is having an unusual experience with the great light and loving radiance of the images that are just as real and meaningful as the warm little goat who occasionally moves to be closer to Naibhu's body. He knows that what he is experiencing is his own lovingness, which has been absent for too long; it was neither the God-man or the baby goat. These were manifest to show him the way—what he has missed throughout his life. He clings to the goat because he knows about goats. He has just found the God-man and is not comfortable with all of that radiance. He can always help with a goat if his emotions get too big for him to handle.

He is hiding the kid under his cloak, so the people in the encampment will not know that he needs to cling to his baby as much as it needs him. Naibhu remains in the shadows, watching the golden leader inside this large domed temple. All of a sudden he changes places with the God-man. Naibhu looks out in reverse, but he keeps the goat in his arms- he does not exchange his precious gift. The goat smells all sweet and new, like fresh blooming life.

He decides to squat down for a while to absorb the gloriously beautiful thing that is happening to him. There are men around the leader as though they are having a special supper together. Naibhu likes that; he never eats at a table. He is transformed. He knows it is not the same as his goat but he knows he is to learn from both. What is being disclosed is to redirect his life. He is closing out the first direction his life has taken and eagerly looking toward the next.

That little black, white and brown, patched up goat comes straight to Naibhu to move him to a new path. Little animals seem to do that to people, often better than people. This little one has information for him. He has known for several days that he is being called to help mankind. He is no longer happy just serving animals. True, he loves animals, but there is something pulling him beyond animals. And yet he does not know how to serve people. In fact, he knows little about humans. He has never had a close relationship with a human being; that is why he knows so little about himself—no one to learn from, no deep and close relationship to another soul. Although he has been a teacher to the children in the farm town for a short time, he really never knew them or anyone else.

He knew the men in the institution the best. He has been a drifter and a rover who does not understand people. Now he has got this great pull towards humans. It is a very strong yearning. Some of this he felt when he went down to the settlement in the woodsy ravine where the migrant workers lived. He had surprised himself when he went around to meet them all. He never had done anything like that before. He visited and had something to say to each one of them.

As he continues to sit on the rocks holding his living bundle of love he realizes a stirring and he does not know how to carry it out. Serve people? The only thing he can do to serve people is to do some physical chore to help them, to carry something for the women, to do something particularly strenuous for the men; that is all he knows. He knows nothing else. He does not really know how to talk to people. Yes, he can communicate because he has words, but he does not know how to talk with people. Just talking with people...he does not know how to do that. If people want something from him or he from them, he can talk easily to them. But the talking to people about themselves and about feelings and knowings and experiences, he does not know how. And he has never talked to anyone about himself either. He has always, always been alone.

Chapter Twenty

He is back on the rock now. He looks around for the "lady" because he wants to talk with her. He never talks much to her; she just stands close by. He remembers all the times when he was a little boy; she was always there. He is afraid that his recent anger will prevent her from coming back to him, but when he calls for her she comes immediately. He tells her that he is lonely, and she tells him to go and find some people, to tell them that he wants to talk with them because he is lonely; they will understand.

Gingerly, he walks down into the encampment where he had not been happy. She tells him to go down and talk with the people; he has a need and so he goes. He tucks his little goat under his arm before starting down the hill to the encampment. He first finds a man and a woman. He crouches down and smiles at them telling them that he has been up in the hills and very lonesome.

He has found this little abandoned goat, and he just wants to tarry a minute and talks with them. They eagerly talk with him, and he feels how nice it is to be in the company of others. He tells them about his little baby goat and how it has lost its mother, how he feeds it and how it stays with him. He finds these people are warm, very quiet, friendly people. They seem to like him and he stays a little longer than he expected he would. They give him something to drink. He bids them good-bye and goes on. He has never remembered doing that with anyone before. Nothing great had taken place, yet something very nice had happened. He feels all warm, and he snuggles up even closer to his little goat. He has learned something, that if he really needs and he is able to share, he can find someone who will share a few moments with him for no reason—if he needed. And he thinks...they must need, too. They must need him. If he needs, they must need. That is how he will learn about humans.

He moves through the village a little farther and finds an old, old lady. She looks sad, very sad. He removes his little goat from under his cloak and shows her how loving it is. He says, "Why don't you hold my little goat?" While he fixes her fire, the little lady holds his baby goat. She gets all soft and warm and smiles as the little goat looks at her and nuzzles up near her chin. He talks to her about the big responsibility to take care of a little one. This sad and ancient one seems to find some happiness. He stays there quite a long time just talking to her. Although he is not saying anything in particular, she is smiling. The cares seem to leave her face as she looks at his little goat and pets and loves it. He is glad to share it with her—a little, loving, trusting thing...that little goat. He goes out and finds some wood for her which he stashes against the tree so she can get it easily in the morning. He asks her if she has someone to care for her. She answers yes; she has a son, but he is away right then. So he moves on as she is growing weary and sleepy.

He picks up his little goat and goes on a little farther

to look for goat milk. He is teaching the goat to lap the milk off his finger. He returns to the rocks where he now sleeps with his goat; he is feeling very happy and full, although there seems to be no reason. Nothing really much has happened except something new. He has never, ever gone up to a stranger just to talk about nothing at all. He feels full of love and he has made some friends. Now he has some new friends. A man and his wife, a little old lady...and a goat! That is a lot more than he had yesterday.

He awakens refreshed in the rocky area, radiated by a very luminescent light. He visualizes himself in a purple robe. It makes little difference that he does not have any kind of robe. But that is how he sees himself, standing very, very tall among his people. He remembers walking into the first city feeling very important. He does not feel important now; he just feels different than he has. He hastens down into the encampment to see his people and to move amongst them as they prepare breakfast, greeting each one and moving on. Later he chooses a spot between the city and the encampment along side the road where he sits with his goat in full view of people walking to their work in the city. They see his peace and radiance and stop to talk with him. They come to tell him about their problems, their needs and concerns. He listens quietly and tells them that they will be taken care of, that what they need they will have. His little goat lies beside his feet. He is in a very glorious state, sitting there in a very, very strong light.

The time passes rapidly for Naibhu. It is as though he has been primed for his new work that he is now apprenticing. He is surprised that many, many people stop without his gesturing or calling them and each starts talking with him first as though they need him. On his way back into the hills, he tones again. He has not toned in a long time. He tones when things are good. When he tones, he hears very high voices singing. He reaches his senses up to join them. There is great apprehension mixed with joy. In spite of all the glory, he has the feeling he is going on a path of no return. He cannot go back. The sound is all around everywhere. He is in awe and he is definitely frightened. He calls out to his little goat as if the goat can help him. He knows he is going toward his destiny. As he stands in the intense light, he is trying to remember. It is coming from all sides, that light; he cannot get away. He cannot even run. He collapses on the ground and he grabs the little goat. Crumpled on the ground, he cries out for the "beautiful lady."

She comes as she has told him that she would whenever he calls. He asks her what is happening to him. She says that God is touching his life. He will feel the glory and beauty. He is in a very high place when he asks her, "What is God?" She answers, "Every man must find his God. Man can only know God through his own experience with God." Naibhu says to her, "But I do not know God." And she says, "As you look within the depths of your soul you will find the greatest beauty which is God. God is man's understanding of the divine creation of the world and all within it. God is man's experience of infinite wisdom. When he harmoniously fuses with the universe while he maintains a thread of separateness, that allows him to help guide the destiny of living things. Some humans experience this God energy in mystical human form. Others see it as an all encompassing essence which directs their lives. Such experiences are profoundly real to all humans at times of stress or overwhelming beauty and love. Then there is universal knowing of the truth of God. At such times of insight, humans realize that their destiny is to choose a path, a way of life that allows these expanded God vibrations into everyday consciousness so that they live and manifest as divine humans. Your destiny is to manifest the God which you find within yourself to mankind."

The "beautiful lady" is teaching him. He is seeing elaborate images but he does not really have information. She answers his question before he asks it saying, "You do not need any information, you have it all. Only when you find it within yourself, can you help others to find it within themselves." He asks her if he does not have to know anything about the Buddha and the temples and all the rituals. She answers, "No, you will teach truth with the purity of primary knowing." He sits there quietly trying to comprehend. He hears the message, all of it and he understands. He does not quite know what to do with it.

Naibhu's body starts to vibrate from toe to head. Waves of energy sweep over him causing his big frame to undulate forward and backward, progressing upward. He excitedly asks what is happening. She quietly answers, "You are tuning up, tuning up. Be quiet and passive, allow the impulses and energy to sweep over you, to cleanse and strengthen every fiber, not to doubt or wonder but to allow—sense and listen to sounds and thoughts particularly." The little goat senses it too and becomes very alert. "If you have something to say, or a message comes to you and no one is around, you must tell it to your little goat. You are moving into the level of vibrations where you can directly communicate with God. God is everywhere, but most humans cannot reach the frequency level where they can comprehend God." He likes what she said about sharing his thoughts. All the things he was learning he would tell his little goat. As if he had to speak it to know it. If it stays inside he would not quite know it or he would forget it.

Naibhu comes into another state now...perhaps in a little bit of shock. He remembers what the "lady" said. He does not have to do anything. He just has to follow all the impulses that come, to trust them and to take note. He remembers he has done that before, at least paying attention before but not like this. In the past when he followed, his life was saved.

He did not always know where he was going but this is somehow different. He understands what she said. This time he is going to follow the light. Wherever it takes him, he will follow the light.

Chapter Twenty-One

Naibhu sits down on the rock and plays with his little goat. He realizes that he has to get a name for him because he calls him and talks with him. The name comes instantly; it will be Juda. Sometimes Juda will come when called; he is such a bouncy, happy being. Naibhu starts his morning, greeting small groups of people with a message for each person. His happiness is extraordinary. They even call out to him and ask him if something has happened. They think he has received some material thing to be so joyful. Although he answers that nothing has happened, something has happened to him. He calls back to them joyfully, the message of happiness radiating from his voice. He moves amongst the people with nothing except his radiating happiness. That is his message.

He comes full circle back towards the north when he has finished his greetings. As he sits among the rocks, he is aware of the fact that he is glowing and radiant, and Juda is prancing around. He comes and stands on his leg and puts his head up toward his face. Juda does not lick Naibhu; he jumps up and bleats and lays his head beside Naibhu's. Even when they sleep, he places his head up to Naibhu's face. He never touches Naibhu's face; he just lies with his head beside it. This man is very happy as he sits in the sunlight. He sits there for a long time in wonderment. The little children come bringing gifts. They do not bring flowers. They bring the little things of their life—their smooth stones, pieces of wood, little grass things that they make, all things that are very important to them. They bring them to him as their gifts. They sit on his lap. He holds and comforts them because many of the children are sad. Their parents are gone all day and they are left alone to play with whatever they can find; their little encampment has nothing for children. They come to him, bringing what they have that is very precious to them. They bring him their little possessions which they tell him about. He loves the children and he talks to them through their very deep sadness. They hear and change.

At first there are only a few little ones that come. Later there are many who come to sit at his feet. They look at him and they listen to him. Juda is out amongst them and he loves them, too. Naibhu moves his sleeping place closer to the village. He has an earthen dish which he takes each morning around to the people to ask for food to feed the children. Often when they come to him in the daytime they are hungry. He brings the food back and places it next to his little altar of rock. If the children come to see him and are hungry, there is always enough food.

When the day is over, Juda has been fed, Naibhu has eaten and the children have all been fed as well. They grow to be happier children, instead of holding the deep sadness that they came in with. They play around him. Where he sits becomes a play yard of the little children who run, laugh and create child like things. Juda becomes a helper...if a tiny child wanders too far away from the older ones, Juda goes after him to bring him back. He gets him by the seat of his pants and tugs upon him until he returns. If they crawl away, Juda goes after them herding them back. Juda is getting bigger now and he is a very determined little goat.

Every day Naibhu has his children. Every day! And when the parents come home at night they know where to find their own—down at the end of the encampment with the goat man, the gentle radiant goat man.

When the parents come, they frequently stay for a while. They stay to pour out their cares. There is little happiness in this group because their lives are purposeless. They trudge; they work and they endure, but they have few comforts or possessions, so they come and pour out their troubles to him. He never gives them an answer although they want answers to solve their troubles; he talks about joy, happiness, light and God. Always they go away feeling better, wondering...who is this strange man?

Each day more people come. More people come to see him, to come close to him, to be with the little children. Naibhu is happier than he can ever remember. It seems strange to him because of its newness, his overflowing happiness goes wherever he goes. Everyday the people come to join their children visiting the goat man. They ask him questions about subjects he knows nothing about. He puts his hand on their heads and he tells them to discover the radiance of God and there will be no problems. He knows something is happening to this whole group of people because of him. Some of them are slow, and they come to sit in the back where they listen but do not participate too much.

Chapter Twenty-Two

Juda is quite a character now, one ear goes up and one ear goes out. When he is listening very intently, he moves those great big floppy ears in different ways that never seem to track. Naibhu tells Juda that they are going to take a little trip back to a place where he used to work. Before he never wanted to go back there, but now he is going back to see his animals, to say good-bye to them because he is going far away. He does not know where he is going, but he knows that this is his last time in this area. He and Juda jaunt along the road, back toward the big city that he had never known or liked. He does want to see his animals that he has not seen in a long time. When he arrives, the men think he has come back to work in the large corrals with the many horses, yaks and camels.

These workmen give Naibhu a hard time, joshing him. Where has he been? He left them to do his work! They look at him and they know that he is somehow changed.

He tells them that he is going away, where he can teach. When they ask him what he is going to teach, he replies that he is going to teach about beauty and about the light and the love of God and he does not know what else. These are funny, hard, cruel men who make fun of him with, "Who are you? You belong out cleaning the stables." It does not seem to affect him very much. He just smiles and says he has found something that he is to share and he is going away to do that. When he starts to go they follow, trailing after him and no longer making bad remarks. They follow him all the way to the end of the corrals. He turns and gives them a blessing, and he tells them to care for those under their charge, the animals, because they too belong to God. He says, "As you care for animals, I will care for people."

He turns and starts down the road again; he thinks of the many roads he has been on, each time leaving one thing, each time never knowing where the next will lead to, but this time he has a living possession—he has Juda.

Juda is always happy and ready to go! He runs ahead as though he is showing the way. Naibhu walks for miles in his drapey clothes and tattered coat, dish in hand and his goat nearby.

He feels that he has a robe about him, a long and flowing robe. Soon he comes to a little temple. He has not been inside a temple for a very long time. He goes inside and finds that it is a Buddhic temple. He sits and he looks at very pretty things with lots of gold and a Buddha. There are people coming and going. He is not very comfortable, for he remembers the big Buddha that he was touching when they found him and took him to prison. Somehow he does not feel good in this temple. It seems so heavy and contained that it depresses him. He stays a while watching the people. He is learning something or formulating something. He requests the presence of the "beautiful lady." Her presence quiets his disturbance. She says that Buddha knows about God not as a man image or guidance from above but as a right view where everything in the universe depends on everything else, giving humans compassion for all. But people have forgotten what Buddha taught. Now they worship Buddha. She tells him that the more things they can put in the temple, the more spiritual they think their temple is. In this way they have lost the essence of the spirit. She tells him, "Go inside yourself to find God." Immediately, he does and there is the light, all over the steps coming up to the temple. The sad people that are rushing in to say their prayers miss the light, so they are just as sad coming out after they have said their prayers. He sees the light and he stands there with deep happiness. It is as though he learns that he does not have to go anywhere to find his God. He does not have to go into that temple, for the temple is not beautiful to him. He stands off to the side of the steps and he watches the people come and go as he thinks. Juda is beside him. The day is magnificent. He stands there and he experiences God. The world becomes so bright that he is lost in ecstasy.

He sees Juda move down the steps toward some little children who have stayed outside as their parents go inside. Juda herds the children as he has learned to do and brings them up around Naibhu. He puts out his hands and touches them. Soon there are more who come. When the people leave the temple, they see him standing there with his little goat and their children. He says nothing but he acknowledges them. Soon the steps are full of people, not going or coming but staying. He blesses them with love and he tells them to take their love and go about their work, sharing it with all living things. He tells them that they will prosper. Naibhu stays there the remainder of the day outside the temple. The people come all day. More and more people come over to him on their way to and from the temple. He stands on the steps to the right of the temple entrance. The temple is not in a city but outside the city near some farm buildings, small and very old. It has everything in it. No matter where he looks, the walls and floor are covered.

People decorated it for years and years. He knows that he has to stay near the temple for several days. When it becomes dusk, he leaves with Juda and goes into a nearby grove of trees to sleep.

He has forgotten about food, but Juda is hungry. The stars come out and he delays sleep, resting and wondering. He does not know where he is going and what is happening. He talks to the "lady" who tells him that as he moves among the people, he will be taught. When the day comes, he goes a short distance up the road to beg for food. He finds people he has seen the day before. They recognize him and put food in his little dish. He thanks them and blesses them and tells them about love. Then he feeds Juda and hurries back to the temple.

The same thing happens that day. As people come and go, more and more of them come especially to be with him. Two priests come and tell him to go...to leave, that he is not a Buddhic priest and he cannot be there on the steps. Naibhu accepts what they say without response. He starts toward the grove of trees and the people go with him. So many people go with him, eagerly. They want something from him, but they don't know how to ask him questions and he does not know how to answer them. They are like children who feel a need but do not know how to ask for what they need. So for several days they sit quietly together. Finally they ask him who he is, why he has come and where is he going? He has no answers to these questions.

As Naibhu talks with them, he tells them a story. It is the story of a man who has spent his life in hardship and who has wandered and wandered looking for something, who has worked close to the land and close to the animals. This man was always cared for and always found his way. But he was also always afraid and always looking. He was always, always searching. No matter how bad things got, he was always searching. When things got better, he was still searching. He tells them about the "beautiful lady" who comes and talks to him when he is depressed. He tells them that he seems to get more depressed the more possessions he has and the harder his life becomes. He tells them he is probably like they are, they work and they work and the more they get, the more they wonder. He tells them that one day when he was so distraught and was reaching for answers, the "lady" came and told him all about God and what God is and where he would find his God. She told him he will find God in his own life and his own experience. God will be a radiance that he has never known and will give him a power that will make all good things happen. She told him that he does not have to search; he only has to look inside and forget what he thinks he is and let his soul tell him his true identity and what he needs.

When he finishes his story the people give him a name, they call him "the shining one." Again that night when the stars come out he does not sleep. He wonders. He asks for the "lady" again to tell him what he is to tell the people the next day. They are so eager and searching. She tells him to tell them that he is a human being who is finding God and that they too are human beings, that do not need to look to the past, they can look to the now and they can find God in their lives.

The next day Naibhu is troubled because he sees that the people are not going into the temple; they are coming to the orchard where he sits. They are coming to see him and not the Buddha. He becomes troubled because the people come and kneel down to him. He goes to put his hands under their chins and raise them up. They are confused because they had learned to bow down to the Buddha.

Some of the great happiness that he has had saddens. He decides that he has to leave this place. He has to leave and go away from the people because there is something wrong. They worship him. He is not quite able to get them to perceive God; they need a Buddha figure. What is happening to these people is not quite right.

That night he and Juda do not go back to the grove. They go back into the hills far away where the people cannot find them. They go up on a small hill which overlooks the land and which is clear of trees. There on the hill, they cannot be seen; that is the way it is to be for some time for Naibhu must straighten out something that he found not right.

He calls in the "lady" who comes in all her beauty, smiling, radiant and well pleased—almost happy that he is confused and troubled. She tells him the hardest thing about his teaching will be the beliefs of the people. Whatever he says, they will relate to what they know and what they believe, and it will be twisted, turned and used. Whenever he knows it is used incorrectly, he suffers. She says that suffering will continue for many years because he will believe that he has falsely taught them.

She asks him to stay on that hill for several days and to go back into the beautiful part of his soul that he has found. As he communes with this part of his being, he will know God more deeply and will be strengthened before he goes back down to the people.

Naibhu follows her teaching as he tells Juda how joyful it is to be alive, so very, very joyful! Every part of him radiates life and vitality. He has always been a very strong man but this is a different kind of strength. This is the kind of vitality that has no limits. It has absolutely no bounds. It permeates everything; it goes everywhere. He is a part of it, and he is so joyful, so grateful. He can hardly remember the deep sadness on the rocks when the "lady" came and got him into trouble again. Now she is with him. It is as though she is his playmate, moving, being and experiencing life with abundance.

Chapter Twenty-Three

As he runs and plays with Juda, the little goat gets hungry. Now the goat eats everything, and so his food is plentiful. Naibhu is not hungry; he is fasting. It is a very light hearted time in which Naibhu is not concerned with food. He cannot remember when he has had such a glorious carefree time with a companion. His heart soars. He feels love for every single thing. This love reaches out as though it covers the entire countryside, spreading into every one, touching every soul. He feels it because it is part of him. He wants to stay this way forever, forever!

He has no need to go anywhere because all of his needs are satisfied. He has found God. His chest is bursting with joy, the kind of joy that he can share with his little goat who walks and runs and brings him things when he sits down. It is as though Juda is offering him something to eat because he knows Naibhu is fasting. He will present him with pieces of wood or an old twig. The days are full of awareness that reaches beyond the grasses, beyond the trees and beyond the birds. He has always been acutely aware of the things very close to him but has never been aware of beyond. Now his awareness is spread all over, to blanket the whole region. His lovingness pours out from him, spreading in all directions. He has more than he can ever use. He shares it abundantly as though it is a cover of protection for the entire land. He sleeps. He tones. He talks to the "lady", and most of all he talks to his God. He loves his little goat Juda who is becoming very wise now. These are the happiest days of his life; he has no unfulfilled needs. He feels a tremendous extension of himself everywhere.

One day the "beautiful lady" comes and tells him he has to go, that he is needed in the village. His people need him. He is reluctant to go because the people have so many worries, so many troubles and he has so few now. He thinks that to go down amongst them would remind him of something that he does not wish to know about. He sits for a long time wondering if he will go. He has found life very, very precious to him. It is so fresh and new it could be tenuous. He cannot leave it; he needs more of it. She has sent him here and now she is calling him away. With great reluctance, he starts down toward the little grove of trees where he last met the people...where he left in the middle of the night. As he approaches this little village, he knows there is something wrong. There is such a heaviness that he longs to run back up into his special cathedral of trees. And yet, he plods down there drawn by the "lady" who says that he must go.

When he approaches, there is no one in the grove. He goes on until he comes to the temple and there is no one in the temple. He turns and heads out on the road going north as his course carries him. Before he travels very far, he comes to a river. The people are on the river banks; there are hordes of people! He stops and wonders why they are there. Someone spies him, hastening and urging him to go down to the river banks to be with his people who are very bereaved. His heart is heavy...his joy leaves him. He wishes to run away and not to continue. But Juda leads the way, so he follows down without asking why. He wonders if Juda knows something that he does not know. Juda goes ahead on a narrow path down to the banks where the people gather.

There is the body of a little boy who has drowned. The two priests who ordered him away from the temple steps are there also. Naibhu holds back. He remembers the goats that died; he knows about death. He always put his hand on the goat's head and talked to it before he laid it to rest. Now he loses Juda in the crowd; he cannot find him and he quickly becomes very upset. He searches for Juda for some time before he sees him down with the little drowned boy. Juda always goes to children in trouble. Naibhu forgives him for not knowing that the boy is beyond trouble.

He moves toward Juda through the crowds of people weeping and wailing; some are toning; some cling to him as he moves on toward Juda. The little boy's body lies on the grass of the river bank. Everything stops. Naibhu stands there frozen! His little goat is stationary and the little boy is dead. There is no action. He hears something behind him and he turns to see a very tiny girl, smaller than the drowned boy. She comes to him and she throws her arms around his leg sobbing deeply. He picks her up and holds her closely, for he knows that this little child saw what has happened. The boy is her brother.

They sit on the grass. He likes grass. The people have moved away into a partial semi-circle. The little girl had crawled out of the circle to come to him. She is no more than two years old. He holds her warmly; he remembers how he used to talk to his goats after they died. Soon he moves closer kneeling down beside the little boy with the tiny girl in his arms, and he tells her that he will talk with him and tell him that they miss him, that he knows he is safe and that they will never forget him.

Naibhu looks up into the hills and the countryside. His deep love spreads everywhere. He is aware of it and he is very thankful for it. The little girl is quiet. Juda is at his feet. He gently presses his hand on the little boy's forehead, and he speaks about love and God. Naibhu's energy keeps expanding outward until he becomes invisible. He is not aware of the God consciousness he is channeling. He loses human identity while radiating a divine light. His work is done, so he tries to rise to go, but he cannot. He slumps on the ground and is lost to the reality of his surroundings. Juda rushes to him, licking his face excitedly. He knows his master needs him to awaken him from wherever he is lost.

After some minutes Naibhu staggers to his feet. Unsteadily he moves back toward the road. He has moved only a short distance when the people rush in surging past him to the river's bank. He moves on, stopping eventually, turning around. Now he can see the people's frenzied excitement. They are helping the little drowned boy to his feet. He lives. The little girl is urging him to return.

Naibhu feels intense fear as if to protect himself from an overwhelming realization. He sees the people in ecstasy, yet some are weeping. He finds Juda and sets his feet in the other direction toward the road. On the road he walks as rapidly as he can in a northerly direction in order to get away. He is afraid that the people will follow him. He is not very stable. He remembers the times he has run away from something; now he finds himself running away again, concerned and confused and more frightened. Something has happened that he does not believe. He goes as fast as he can go. Juda runs beside him. Juda knows. Soon he has left the little township far behind and he is alone again.

He seems to be carrying a very heavy burden. All of his light heartedness is now gone. Before he played and was free, and he sent his love all over this land. He does not understand why everything is burdensome. He remembers the people and their emotions and the agony on their faces. He remembers the little girl's sobbing. He wonders where she is. He walks on and as the sun is setting he gets off the road. He crawls into a little lean-to structure; apparently for animals at one time but now there are no animals there. He needs the shelter for its protection. No one will find him.

He sits and weeps. He calls for the "beautiful lady" to come and help him to understand. She tells him that these people understood what has happened. When Naibhu touched the boy's head, life had returned. The little boy was given back to the people to show them the light and to bring them joy. These people have been so sad because they have lost some of that light. They are crying mostly for themselves. They do not understand that the little boy's light will never go out. God had decided that his light was needed, so the light had returned. Naibhu brought the light of God back to the child. He asks the "lady" more questions about things he does not understand. He intuitively understands that God can restore life, but he does not understand the people—why they cry and then are so joyful—almost beyond themselves.

The "beautiful lady" tells him that when the people saw the boy's dead body, this activated their own great urge to live, and the preciousness of physical existence. They responded with deep sadness, depression and mourning. Suddenly, when the boy's life returned, their emotions changed to elation and disbelief. Yet they struggled to understand why, now that he is alive again, their emotions shift back and forth between joy and ecstasy to sadness with sobbing. The "beautiful lady" tells him that confusion is inevitable when feelings are restricted to an understanding of death and life of the physical body. She adds that this dramatic incident in the lives of people is one of Naibhu's big lessons. She tells him that he is to bring to people new understandings of life and death, where sadness would be tempered by the realization of the greatness of the God-plan for the development of the human soul, where it must transcend the material reality of physical existence in its quest for divinity.

She tells him that his second great learning is that he

is a co-creator with the God energy. "Naibhu, it is not you alone who performs this miracle of life from death, but you are part of the divine plan for humans to comprehend the spiritual strength which is theirs to manifest." She adds, "God is well pleased with you." He experiences a jolt in his consciousness. He reaches out for his humanness by holding his little goat as the tears spread over his face. The "lady" continues softly, "This level of teaching is your destiny."

Chapter Twenty-Four

He sleeps amazingly well. When he awakens, his little playmate is frisking around as if to remind him, "We have got a lot to do today and let's be about it." He marvels at the little animal's energy. While he has been quite exhausted, this little one is full of life. He knows it is a fresh, new day and that something he has learned will probably always be with him. He has learned about people and about death. He wonders about those funny little smoking pots that the priests swing back and forth. They are held by ropes. He wonders what these are for.

He starts out following Juda who seems to know where they are going. They go north again. Some of the heaviness of the past is lifting and he feels his feet on the ground for a change. He is moving along really gently, kind of hopping along. It is a glorious day. He tones softly; everything is nice.

Along comes a cart with some oxen pulling it. The man asks him if he wants a ride in the hay. He has never had a ride in the hay—ever. He accepts the ride and picks up his little goat. He crawls into the cart and just lies there in the hay, very proud, looking at the sun. He does not care where he goes; everything smells so good. The little goat is happy. The little cart does not fit him. He laps over the foot of it. He lies there dreaming and watching the world turn back into a beautiful, rosy state. He loves everything again, including the load of hay and the man and the oxen.

The man comes to his destination and tells Naibhu that this is as far as he goes. He asks Naibhu where he is going and Naibhu says he does not know; he is just going. The man invites him to stay and have some food; his little goat will be watered and fed. Naibhu is amazed because he does not know this man. He has never seen this man and he has not asked him for anything. He is hungry, but he does not say anything to the man about food. Somehow the man knows he is hungry and he asks him to come in where his wife has food prepared.

He sits at their table and he eats. He has never done that before. He has never sat at a person's table because they want him to eat with them. He is absolutely glowing. The man goes out and calls some friends from nearby to come and see this big man that he has found on the road. The people come in, and he sits and talks to them, telling them how beautiful the world is. As he talks, he exudes happiness. Juda is outside with lots of other little goats.

They want Naibhu to stay. They have some work for him. He thanks them warmly and declines; he has to be on his way. They ask him what he does and he answers that he talks with people. There are lots of people he is supposed to talk to and so he has to be going. He will talk to people wherever people are and whenever they ask him to talk with them.

Before he leaves they give him something. They bring him a robe which they put around his shoulder. It is brown and soft, not fancy but fairly new. He asks where the robe comes from and they tell him that a priest had left it. They always wait for him to come back and get it, but he never comes. Now Naibhu has a robe. He asks why he should have the robe, and they say that he reminds them of this priest that came to visit that they never saw again.

So he leaves this little farm area with its special house which is not a shanty with a lean-to but a real house. His goat is happy and he walks very tall. He is trying to get used to the flow of the robe. He likes it but it is—well, he does not know; anyway he walks on. He is full of so much love for these people that shared with him. People he has never met and never known share with him. People come from everywhere to know him and to talk with him. He and his little goat move on. He is a sight in his robe covering up his old cloak—his old black coat that he got somewhere, with the torn off tail that he had used to feed his baby goat. And he moves on.

He is not quite sure about his life. He feels a lightness because now he has a robe about him. He likes the robe, but he feels that it is also heavy. He decides he will take the robe off. That will be a lot easier. He takes the robe off and he carries it. Now he feels better and lighter, but every now and then he looks at the robe to see if it is still there. And on he goes.

He sees many people, for on this road they are coming and going—all busy people, carrying loads and leading live animals. He sees one old man sitting by the side of the road. This one is a very ancient man with gnarled legs. He stops to sit beside him, laying his hand on his knee as he talks to him about the beauty of life. The old man tells him that life is not beautiful; it is very burdensome and he is very tired. He says that he is going toward his family home which is up the road and he is too tired to reach it. Naibhu tells him that he will take him. He is big and strong, and this man is small and light. He will just pick him up and take him. So he does. He picks him up and puts him on his back with the withered legs around his waist. Now he has a dear little old man on his back who wants to go home.

He goes quite a long ways and as he goes he tones. His toning comforts the little old man. Strange that the man changes; he is no longer a burden. He becomes lighter and lighter every mile Naibhu carries him. He carries the tired and beaten old man for quite a long ways. Life seems to come back to him. The closer they get to his home, the more excited the man gets and the more he talks. Finally, they come to his home where he lived long ago.

Some of his people still live there. Now he is home. He has come home to die. He had thought he would die before he got there. He is so joyful, he is practically screaming as Naibhu puts him down. This little old man now stands very straight. There is such joy taking place between two people as though something big has happened—but it has not. He has just carried the little man who does not weigh anything for a short distance to bring him home. The man blesses him and asks him to come in which Naibhu does.

He sits and watches. He sees so much radiance in the little children and the young people at the return of this man. Gradually, without notice, he creeps out of the door. He is full of what is happening inside the house. His little goat is waiting for him at the doorway. They move on in joy. He thinks that the old man's last days will be happy ones.

That night as he beds down just off the road, he takes out his robe which has been rolled up under his arm and he puts it over him and the little goat. He calls the "lady" to come. When she appears, he tells her that he is a happy man. He remembers back on the rocks, way back, when she came and told him that he was to start fulfilling his destiny. He wants her to know that although he does not know what his destiny is yet, he is grateful for his days and the learning.

He seems to be having the first glimpses of the true source of all his concerns and likewise those of the human race. He is experiencing his humanness on two extreme and opposite levels—the mortal and immortal.

He is never quite able to bring both together into the full uninterrupted span of his consciousness. His soul is not yet integrated.

Chapter Twenty-Five

He is walking along with Juda on a very small road with farmhouses along the way. There is not much on his mind. He comes to a turn and sees a small girl. She is sobbing deeply as though her little heart is broken. Naibhu hesitates, realizing he knows nothing about little girls. He has never been close to a little girl. He goes off to the side to comfort her. He picks her up and puts her on his lap. He has only held one little girl child before, the one whose brother drowned. She is such a little one and she is so delicate. He puts his arms around her ever so gently and asks her what has happened. She tells him that she has lost her little dog. The dog has died. This is the only thing she has had to play with because there are no children. She puts her arms around his neck and her face against his as he holds her very gently. He is touched by the child's need. He is not used to her delicateness. He feels her little arms around his neck. She has dark, wet eyes and black hair, such a beautiful child. The only other girl he remembers is his mother, whom he does not remember very well. He holds her and lets her sob. She tells him that she lives with her mother and an old grandfather who work all of the time just to get enough food. She has nobody to play with now.

Juda crawls up and he puts his head right in her lap. When he looks at her with his big eyes, she stops crying. She puts her arms around Juda. Naibhu is so moved that she loves Juda that he tells her she can have him for her own new playmate. He tells her that Juda will take the place of her little dog. Juda will follow her around and be with her always. He is a very good playmate who is happy and likes to romp.

He watches the little girl and the little goat love each other; then he stands up and takes her by the hand. They walk a ways until they come to her house. Then he bids them both good-bye and watches them run off together. Juda turns and starts back, but Naibhu tells him that he is to stay with her. Juda turns back and seems happy to have a little girl to play with.

Naibhu walks on a little ways before he sits down. He weeps like the child wept, for he has given away the only thing he has ever loved. He remembers Juda as a new infant goat who found him and was hungry. He taught him how to suck milk from his finger. He remembers all the times, how devoted Juda was, how loving and how much comfort he gave him.

Naibhu wonders what is happening to him because Juda is the last thing he would have thought he could give away. His goat was the only thing he had, but he gave him away to a little girl who needed him more than Naibhu does. Somehow he is torn between his own needs and something that is very much larger than that, the needs of a little girl and a little goat and the love they felt for each other and the love that he felt for both.

The "beautiful lady" comes and says, "You are to learn that you are not to love a thing. You are to love mankind and all human things. You cannot be tied to a possession or material love, you must go beyond that." She says,

"Your gesture of giving away your most treasured possession reaches beyond object love and now you are caught up with the human emotion of loss." Naibhu has never gathered objects or things; he has not needed anything, but this goat taught him how to love and that was different. Somehow he knows that he has moved beyond object love. The love of God has made him give away Juda, and in giving away his greatest love, he experienced the highest level of humanness. True, he experiences a loss. He has lost a friend—there would be no little goat to talk to or to take care of. He has only himself now. Juda had taught him as much as he would teach his new girl playmate; then she will know as Naibhu knows. Animals are here for such reasons. He remembers Juda with great affection, funny little goat, all knowing, all curious, who has led him many places and has taken him on a path that he probably would not have taken without him.

He finally takes his robe from under his arm and puts it on. He starts again, somewhat saddened. He has no regrets, but there is an empty hole that he knows will be filled. He walks on in the robe of a priest standing tall, wondering where he is going. He does not have his goat to show him, to take him to a little boy who has been drowned or a girl who is alone. He will have to find his path alone. He is not feeling too secure about this, for his goal is not very clear.

Naibhu has been a long time without food which he used to remember because Juda had to be fed. Now he does not have to feed him, so he keeps walking. It becomes dark and he does not stop. He goes on and on. Finally, he finds a farmhouse that has an old lean-to nearby. In it is some hay where he decides to bed down for the night. He knows that he has made another soul very happy that day. He feels real good about that. Still he is very lonesome. Hasn't he been lonesome all of his life? A great urge to be with people comes over him. Now that the goat is gone, he needs people even more intensely. He must find some people. Occasional people that pass are not enough. His need is very strong. He needs his people to teach and care for. He wonders where he will find them. Before he sleeps, the "beautiful lady" comes back and tells him that in a very short time he will find his people...in a very short time. His sleep is full of love and warmth and good dreams because he somehow knows that he will find his people, and he is not to roam and roam and roam the rest of his life; he will stop his roaming and do something good in this life. As he sleeps, he sees a great light and he reaches out to it.

He awakens early in the morning very hungry and eager to go where he is to go. He sees a small temple in the distance. It is far ahead of him, like a mirage at the edge of a hill. It is white. Naibhu walks very fast. He walks very rapidly for a long ways. Occasionally, he greets people on the road, but he does not stop. He has to get there and fast. He is compelled to get there.

When he arrives, he looks at the temple that is all crumbling and falling down. It has not been used for ages. He rushes up the steps. Before entering he falls down on his knees and thanks God for this temple where he knows he will teach. No one comes or goes, not as in the other temples he has seen. He walks into an ancient and crumbling temple. He looks around. It has some faint paintings on the wall, some old statues in the corner, but there is no Buddha, no Buddha at all. There is a small altar of stone, but it is bare. It is very beautiful, regal and simple; he could fix it up. He will make everything beautiful again. The people and he will make it look like new.

He has not eaten for two days, but he is feeling so glorious he wants to fast. He wants just to stay there, to experience that old temple and everything that it has ever been to people. It is a charming old temple, the greatest temple he thinks he has ever seen. It has a kind of purity that seems to be lost when decorated with so much stuff. Yet it is falling apart...deteriorating. He remembers the little town where he lived with loving people whom he taught about goats and about farming.

They did not know about God...but still he remembers the great happiness he has had teaching. He knows it will be like this all over again. Here he can live and teach his family. He is sure nobody wants the old temple, or they would have done something with it. He wants it. This is what the "lady" has told him he will find and nearby will be his people.

That night he sleeps in his own temple. Not like the one he was thrown out of ... or the one he was found in and imprisoned, but his own. One that he will build into a great temple for people. He is totally surrounded with magnificent music.

Chapter Twenty-Six

That night he sleeps in the temple. He awakens early in the morning and he notes the temple is full of birds. In fact, the birds have been nesting in the temple for a long time. He knows the birds have to leave. They can come in, but they are not to live there. He explores the temple and finds there is a small room on both sides of the altar. He chooses the north room for himself because it is cooler. This small room has a doorway without a door and a small window. It is painted white. Both rooms are alike. There is an old piece of wood jutting from the wall where he hangs his robe. This is his first home in a building.

He has slept in some barns, but this is his home. Out the back door, he sees a rolling, hilly country and he experiences its beauty. He goes out the door to look. There is an old well that must still be used because there is a clean path to it. It must still serve water right where it is needed to clean the temple.

Back in the temple, he starts looking around. There

are two dusty statues, one on each side of the front. One is a standing woman of gray stone. He has heard of the lady goddess, the Kuan Yin whom Buddha discovered. He wonders if this is she. At the base of the statue are carved flowers. She stands in the flower garden. Naibhu likes that. On the other side is another statue of the same lady who is kneeling down to comfort a small child.

He is very touched by the ancient statues that he seems to know. As he sits between them for a long time suddenly he knows who she is. She is the same lady he knows as the "beautiful lady" carved in stone. He has known her since he was a child when he ran away from the caravan and was frightened. It was she who held him that first night and who has since directed his life. Naibhu is excited. Now he asks the mystical "beautiful lady" to come to him. She appears rapidly as she always does these days. She tells him that she is depicted in the stone statues for people who cannot contact her directly as Naibhu does. She adds that people make statues to remind them of the higher things that they forget in their every day life. She says it is all right because the statue is symbolic and makes it easier for them to contact these higher teachers. She warns him to help his people, never to treat her as a goddess to substitute for the divine but to use her vibrations to reach the divine.

She tells him he will now begin his destiny as teacher and priest for he has found his temple. His first work is to meet his people. Excitedly he rushes out toward the well to pick some wild flowers that he has seen. There by the well he finds an old broken piece of a crock that holds water. He brings in the flowers and places them at Kuan Yin's feet. He thanks her for bringing him to this place, and he says he will follow her instructions and always provide flowers for her.

He puts on his robe and goes out of the temple, to sit on the steps in the sun and to await the people. As they move down the road they see a tall man in a robe sitting on the temple steps. They stop because he is a stranger. He moves out to greet them and to tell them that he has come to repair their temple, to work with them. Everyone seems very happy. They ask him where he comes from and he responds, "From the south, the big city to the south." They ask him his name and he hesitates. He has not used his name and has almost forgotten it. All day long he sits in the sun, greeting the people who pass on the road, telling them his name and that he has been sent to fix their temple.

Early the next morning he is sitting with Kuan Yin, asking where he should start. He notices that the temple is made of stone blocks with a plaster over the inside and outside, and this is cracked and falling off. There is a little round dome in the middle, high up with open sides where the birds perch. It has a wooden frame under it in a criss-cross shape. One wall of the temple near the ground has a huge hole where stone blocks have crumbled. The floor is covered with bird droppings, dust, accumulated straw and dead branches. It seems like a monumental job to restore his temple. But to Naibhu the work is his pleasure. He has planned to do it all by himself as he has always done. Even if he does not know one thing about building or repairing a structure, he thinks he will figure it out. He starts cleaning out the junk inside and the fallen blocks. He stacks the debris neatly away from the building. This brings much curiosity from the people, even more than the previous day when he announced he would restore their temple.

Soon people who walk the roads with their animals come to talk with him. Excitedly they volunteer their help and several men say they know how to restore the walls. In the days to come, people appear from everywhere, a whole farming community. They do not want him to do any of the work; he is to direct it. This is the way they want it to be. This also is the first time in his life people have said to him, "No, you are the leader, you direct and we will do the work." Usually he is the one doing the work. Now it is the other way around. He feels this way of doing things is strange. Only once in a while when things are very heavy will he step in to lift something into place or push something where it is supposed to be. They are then aware of his great physical strength.

Naibhu watches them intently. They bring the material for repair, goat milk, eggs, straw, manure and sand from the creek bed. They stir a thick plaster-like substance by mixing straw, milk, egg white, manure and sand. Then with their hands, they throw it into the cracks and smear it smooth with their fingers. He has never seen anything like this, people mold this soupy mixture to fill in cracks and repair the wall. He gets so excited, he asks to go fetch the manure; that is his specialty, moving manure.

After they patch the cracks and broken plaster, they start on the dome and the big hole in the wall. The steps, too, have to be reset. Another group of men come bringing clay and sand from the stream bed. They mix these with straw, manure and water, and form bricks.

These bricks are different from the original stone, but when dry, set into place and covered with plaster, these fill the large holes and look the same.

Next they bring rough boughs from trees to repair the little round dome structure. First they bring long poles which they tie together to make a structure high enough to reach the dome. Two men scramble to the top where they bend thin wood in all directions and stick it into the walls reforming the dome structure. Over this they spread plaster with their hands.

He desperately wants to climb up to that dome with them; they look so lofty up there, but he is too big; everything will fall down. These men are small, slender people who scramble up to the dome like little spiders on a web.

Naibhu does not have anything to do with the building except to sit there. He is ever so happy. Even the birds are singing. Just being with these busy, skillful, joyous people is enough; he is watching a temple, his temple, being repaired, constructed before his eyes. This is almost overwhelming to him. It is a miracle—an absolute miracle, that takes him to a lofty state.

He thinks that the only thing he brings to these people is himself. He does not know a thing about repairing a temple. He wonders why they never repaired their temple before. They know all about how to repair the temple, to put it back together. He watches it being put back together by people who will find a new meaning within under his teaching.

He does some work. He repairs the well. That is his work...to straighten the old well. It is a deep well...a very deep well. The old rocks at the top which are not held by water are tumbling down. He goes out and he gets more rocks from the fields, good hard rocks. He takes their plaster stuff and he puts the rocks together. It sticks things well. So he slops his hand in the plaster like the men do. He is actually positively intrigued putting the stones together. He fits them carefully and makes it pretty, too. He has found some colorful rocks, some pink and red which he puts in occasionally.

Every day these people return. Sometimes different people come, all running around...busy young men, old men. He notices that these are a different type of people from the people he has worked with in the first farm village. These are a lot more spiritual and warm, more evolved people.

The temple becomes a hub where people congregate. They come to look and to see what is going on. They bring wood and supplies. He just sits there and talks to each one. He is excited because he notices that he brings something to them while they teach him how to fix the temple.

They bring him some hay which he puts back in his little room. He now has a good straw bed, and they bring him food to eat which he has never tasted before. He gets more food than he needs. He will save it to feed the people who work there. When they get hungry, he has something for them to eat. He sits on the side of the hill to the south of the temple, a very fine place where he can survey everything and see the temple against the land.

They bring some little plants to put around the temple. Every day he carries water to these new plants. He soon learns people's names and about everyone in the community. Kuan Yin has told him this is the first work. Some of the people are so young, they do not know anything about a temple because it has not operated for a long time. This is something very new to them.

Someone comes and washes the gray off of the Kuan Yins. They become a creamy white like marble. Her face is very beautiful; her clothes are not well defined but her face is everything. He goes every day to sit with the Kuan Yin. He is so happy. She is always there in spirit too. He has his own home, a little room; he has food and he has love. He has said to them that he has come to repair and build back their temple. But lots of people are doing things because he encourages it; he does not do anything but he is there. In between times, he goes to the people. He wants to see how they live, to see their farms and so he goes. These are good farms not poor ones. These are better farms than he has ever seen with lots of healthy animals. They are busy people, strong people and they seem to be happy people. He needs this kind of people so badly.

They take him in as if they know he has been sent. Some of them say that they knew when he was coming. They have been told he is coming, that he is a big young man. Years before the temple housed a very old priest but he did not serve the people so they drifted away. Now Naibhu does not know what he is supposed to do except when the time comes, he is to start teaching these people.

Now he is just becoming one of them. Actually he seems to back away from his next teaching work. He knows it is full of emotions. He is not too comfortable. The work of rebuilding is nearly complete. The beautiful Kuan Yin is around; he has a home, a place to stay; he has food; he has the warmth and the love of people who have been looking for him. They have been looking for him as if they prayed all the time for someone to be sent to them. He is having trouble because he has another role other than to visit with people at their farms and spend the day talking, and yet he seems to need this. This other role is the one he would like to delay. He even hopes it will take them an awfully long time to get the temple built...to get it all done. It is almost as though he would like this way of life just to continue...it occupies everybody's time and interest. It is a building, a very material thing, but as it nears completion, he becomes anxious. He has all of the beauty and all of the joy that he ever wanted, even a family. He has all of it. He has total acceptance from everyone, the oldest one to the youngest one. They were prepared for him because they knew he was coming. They have been looking for him for a long time. They tell him that his name means the "awaited one." This makes his responsibilities more overwhelming.

Chapter Twenty-Seven

Now it seems to be a time of preparation. The temple is nearly complete. It is all new and white again. Inside it has a rosy glow to it. They leave little slits in the round dome where light comes through. It comes down and reflects all around the temple. Whatever direction the sun, it always brings that pink color into the room. The floor is clean, very polished rock. It has been polished by many, many feet that have trod into this little temple. The whole temple has a soft kind of majesty to it.

Naibhu goes every day, early in the morning after he puts on his robe, to the main temple room. He goes to talk to the Kuan Yin; she is teaching him. He now has two little clay vases to hold the flowers. He picks flowers every morning, bright and early when the dew makes them fresh. The first day he picked them, his hands were very clumsy. He has seen flowers since he was a little boy up in the mountains, and he has lain amongst flowers in the spring with the goats. He loves to see flowers, but he has never thought of picking them. Now he places fresh flowers at the foot of the Kuan Yins each day.

He goes into this lovely little temple now with its soft polished floor. They cleaned out the dirt and the polished floor is there; it has a rosy glow. As the sun comes up in the east and goes around to the south of the temple to set in the west, there is always a rosy glow in that room coming from the floor.

He sits quietly and he starts toning again. He has almost forgotten how to tone. He remembers the mown hay where he has slept, where Kuan Yin came to him to comfort his nervousness about impending danger. He remembers the instruments that the people loaned him to play and how he toned to the sounds of the instruments. His voice was clumsy then and again it is clumsy now. But now is his practice time. In the morning he tones very softly. Somehow in this little temple it is different than toning in a hay mow. In the hay mow when he tones it just goes away. In this little temple, it comes back again, again and again, from all sides and from the top. So it is really a lovely, lovely thing for him to hear later. He stops and listens to the tones as they come from various places. And so he practices toning, just allowing the sounds to come out. It gets better and better every day. In the early evening after seeing the people he goes into the temple and tones again. The little children come in to hear the sounds. They move up behind him and sit on the floor looking at the Kuan Yins. They tone with him. They understand toning; it is so natural to them. Their little voices join with his big, big voice. He sits there by the hour sometimes and he just tones. The messages come to him that this is his preparation, his tuning to be a priest and bring God's message.

The temple is nearly done and the children are the first to come to it regularly. In the afternoons, they are waiting for him. He puts on his robe and comes from his back room, out around the side of the building to the front door where he takes the children in with him. He leads them into the temple. He never says anything to the children. The children apparently take something back to their homes, which interests the older ones.

The remainder of his day he spends with the people. They only know how to plant or grow things. He shares and talks with them about life, and he makes many friends. They come looking for him, but there is no particular role he has and he does not give them information. They do not come to the temple regularly. It has not been a part of their life for long. It is as though there is a part of them that knows about the meaning of a temple, but they just poke their heads inside and then go on. It is not a pattern in their lives to come to this temple. They are pleased with what they have done. They like it. But it is with the little children that he starts his teaching, and he teaches them by toning. There are no words. God comes to little children by sound, by the vibrations of love carried on every tone.

Naibhu is a bit sad. He loves the people and especially the little children. He is willing to help in any way, but he is not needed as much as he has been in the other little towns. He spends more time inside the temple asking God what he is to do and how he is to do it? He is supplied with everything, a place to live in a temple, little children every day and bigger group to talk with but he does not receive any teaching messages. No one tells him what to do or how to do it. His life has everyday peacefulness and beauty. How could he be so sad? He has the urge to move on. They told him he is the "awaited one," and yet no one seems to know why he is awaited. For whatever is to happen in this little temple...apparently the people are not ready and neither is he. Nothing happens.

Every day he tones. Every day the children come. Life is so easy for him and the people. The crops grow; the animals live, breed and multiply. The children are healthy and happy. There is plentiful food and there is happiness for plenty, but he is very sad. His life is easier, simpler and better than he can ever remember. He is warm and full, he has everything that he needs, all of the people, the goodness, a cover over his head—a beautiful temple, the Kuan Yins, flowers and little children.

He experiences a heaviness like a black cloud descending. He believes a disaster is about to hit this community, and he does not know what it is. There is some impending danger! He is very restless and awake much of the night. He spends more and more time talking to the Kuan Yin because he does not know what kind of danger is coming or how to help the people.

His mind is searching for what is coming, what is going to hit the land. He thinks he can ward it off if he knows what it is, but he does not know what it is, so he is caught in a state of anxiety. Even his toning changes.

Finally his foreboding is realized. Some kind of pestilence comes into the community making the people sick. They have been such healthy people and now in a few days many are not well. He goes to the people. They suffer from an acute dysentery. Their symptoms are not new to these people as dysentery has always been around, but not like this. Their stomachs swell and they become very frail. The little ones are worse.

Naibhu does not know anything about sickness. He knows about crippling because many workers injure themselves. He is overwhelmed when these healthy people all become ill. The farms and animals start to suffer. He tears around feeding animals and taking care of things. He is overwhelmed when he realizes the people cannot help. He is so busy and tired at the end of the day, he just falls in his hay bed. He has cared for animals and for people spread out over the whole community. He cannot keep up with the work, and the people are not improving. The drought comes and there is not much water. The fields are very dry and brown. The animals get very skinny and people get sicker. The food is short. The little children do not come back to the temple any more. When Naibhu has time, he tones alone. It is very sad. He talks to the Kuan Yin but he cannot hear her answer. He does not even see her. He cannot understand why his beautiful life has changed to sadness.

All manner of ideas pop into his thoughts but his imagery is muddled and he does not trust what he thinks. He is having a very confused time. He is nervous, worried and does not understand. He tries to talk to Kuan Yin and God but he gets no answers. There is something happening in his mind that is very confusing. He is nervous, worried and does not understand. He tries to recover something as he moves back to remember parts of his life when he seemed to be clear. He searches. He talks with the people but they seem as confused as he is. They are panicking because they cannot go back in the fields and many of them are dying.

He buries dead animals, and sometimes people too when they are the last of the family. He spends a lot of time digging holes. He has not even had time to go up and put his hands over the eyes of the goats and talk to them before he buries them. He is very angry with God because he does not understand. He asks God to help him with the goats and with the people but nothing changes. He just buries more goats. The people are not eating much and they have no strength to feed the animals. As the animals die, they eat some of them but they are so scrawny, it would have been a blessing to kill them earlier. There are no animal babies, so there is no goat's milk, The stench of dead animals is awful. He works all day to bury them. There are so few people in this village who are able to come and dig holes. When the people eat, they retch and have diarrhea as they get weaker and weaker.

This illness moves like a phantom all over the land. There is no rain. The heat is extraordinary, parching the land. This is the most desolate thing he can remember. The land is barren. The trees are dying. The animals are dying and the people are dying. He asks for help, but he does not get it. Somehow he perseveres. He is not ill like these people, except he is so tired. He has asked for this beautiful world where he can teach and he found it. Now it is desolation. The hills are brown and the people have no hope.

Chapter Twenty-Eight

He seems to be lost and at wit's end. He has worked to exhaustion, yet he sees no way out. He is very depressed; his people are dying. He does not want to be there. He has seen them burn a pyre; the people wailed and he "spaced out." He has never seen this before in his life. He knows what to do with goats; he buries them, but he hasn't known what people do with dead bodies. Now he knows that people burn them in a big fire.

Food is very scarce. He refuses food, giving it to the children, although it is not very much. There are no carts moving up and down the road. Everyone is staying quiet and conserving their energies. Whatever this dysentery is, it is lingering. People are waning away; they do not die immediately. They just get slowly worse until they die.

Finally Naibhu takes to his straw bed. He has never been sick in bed before. He has a high fever. A little boy comes to bring him water from the well. He drifts in a stupor. He does not move into the temple; he just lies there, both very ill and exhausted. He has worked all day and into the late night, carrying food around to people, taking care of the few animals in this large community. It is very desolate. Now he remembers his people and he tries to get to his feet. But instead he falls back into his little straw bed where he loses track of time. He remembers sometimes thinking it is dark and sometimes light. He is very hot. He floats away, never moving for hour after hour. There is no contact with the world. A young boy comes off and on to cool his brow with fresh water from the well. He speaks quietly, offering his help. Naibhu is unaware.

After several days Naibhu drifts closer to awareness. He wants to hear a human voice as though this would bring him back from that "no world." He weakly summons the Kuan Yin. For the first time in many weeks, he sees his mystical lady. This time he does not ask any questions; he wants to talk even if incoherently. He experiences two planes of consciousness. One is trying to get command over the other, the speaking one over the drifting, looking one. His throat is very dry. One Naibhu is watching the other Naibhu down there on his bed from a position up in the top of the temple. He is aware of both Naibhu's simultaneously, two streams of awareness coexisting. They are colored differently; the one on the hay is burnt red; the one flying is bright purple—like two energies, the life force and the spiritual force. They do not seem to go together, the red one is stationary while the other moves and drifts around. Then he sees a burning pyre. His body color changes from burnt red to flaming orange. Life is returning to Naibhu. A part of him is becoming aware and a part does not want to experience anything—or to come out of this dual state.

He just lies there caught up in a cycle that perpetuates itself. He does not know what is occurring or how to change it. Then he seems to know what is happening. He is in touch with the deepest, deepest part, his soul. It wants to go. There are so many wrongs that he does not want to stay here. But he cannot seem to go either direction. He is in limbo. He hears; he does not feel or know. In this state nothing seems to touch him; although he hears, he cannot respond. Sometimes he is going up, way up somewhere, where something big will happen. He is afraid of it so he loses consciousness again. He leaves the temple in his awareness for somewhere far out there. He takes nothing with him and he does not plan to come back.

Naibhu can register his feelings, but he is without motivation; he has no will power to work with or to control what is happening. He is in a state of two streams of thought that are unrelated, a void, a drifting void that does not go anywhere—a state of in between. He is not connected to his body; he is hanging suspended, knowing nothingness. It has no being, no information, no substance and it has no urge to move. It is very enticing by its full absentness as if it will stay that way forever. There will be no responsibilities. There will be no concern about goats, people or pain or himself or the world. He is totally relieved of all purpose. There is something else. There are no emotions in this state, absolutely no emotions. It is a free state, free of everything—free of feelings, free of commitments, free of responsibilities, free of toil, free of happiness, free of life, free of humanness, and it stinks. Naibhu knows that to him it stinks.

He does not know if he will come from that state but it is becoming intolerable to stay there. He thinks he will stay there a bit longer before he decides for sure. Then he finds he is looking around at a world he has left, a temple, a straw bed and an open door. Then he thinks he has heard a little girl in the distance. But before he is clearly aware, his consciousness takes off again. It does not go so far. He only goes out in the community to take a look at his people. This is easy; he can check on everything without exhausting himself by going.

This experience is like a change in direction of the pull of the earth to things—not downward but outward, expanding the consciousness until it is gone from the body, dissolving like mist. It seemed to have lost the slender cord which attached consciousness to the physical body. Now he comes to ordinary consciousness, still with these strange memories but now his decision is made. He will live and work and be the big young priest that he is. The mystical lady is there to secure him and to teach him. She says that he has had the most profound learning about himself and humans, that will take days to completely understand. She tells him that he has experienced the secession of the "will" where the "will" is absolutely dormant. There is no "will" to go anywhere, to see anything or to do anything. His soul is locked in the middle as in a trap where his awareness is not high. It is way out away from him, not up. That is very different. Generally the radiating aura around the body is in touch with the body. During Naibhu's experience as the consciousness moves out, the aura lifts from the body surface, with a space in between, not connected with the physical body, until it is nearly a foot away. The colors of light radiating from a living body became cloudy like fog as these separated from his body. Naibhu knows that he has truly experienced the suspension of his "will", the part of him which musters his energy and directs it to do something. His "will" had been very, very strong throughout his life, a "will" that had gotten in his way many times. There was fever; there was physical illness, but the experience which he had was one of almost a lack of movement. His vibrations did not increase very high except they were not low. It was not like an out of the body experience—which he has had many times and had no problem with. This experience was like a change in direction of an attraction; the pull downward of things to the earth now was not downward but outward, expanding the consciousness until it left the body. Dissolving like a mist, disintegrating into nothingness. Consciousness seems to have lost the slender cord to the body, to the things of the world, and there was no controlling "will" to bring it back. He is not in the divine level, not in the near death space. He is in that place of nothingness with no experience and no dedication to move into new directions. This cessation of the "will" is a coma. The "will" is probably a directional aspect of the human field that determines where the person puts his energies. The directions of the transactions with the world, as well as with self, are also in abeyance. This experience would help Naibhu to understand the "will" as a source of man's strongest behaviors. Naibhu, the man, did not have the strength or the wisdom to find his way back. It was a state in which only the soul could choose. For a while a choice has been made and it was a choice which had no movement; it was totally stationary without directed action. Naibhu wonders if this kind of deep knowing came to him to teach him the depth of humanness as he prepares for his mission.

He finds himself lying on the bed of hay, coming to a state of awareness of the real world. He has been very ill. Gradually he arises weakly, not knowing how long it has been since he has eaten. It seems that there is no more fever. He is weak as he moves gently to the door and holds on. He sees the same parched land that he has seen before and yet there is less grayness now. There is a darkness to the sky indicating that rain is imminent. He goes out to get some water. There are a few wild flowers which he picks for the Kuan Yin. She has not had flowers for days. He puts on his robe and he goes into the temple. There he sits, quietly aware that his "will" is back with him. It is not strong and it is not full of the fire that it usually has. And it is not as tightly connected to his body, to his physical life as it had been. It has a greater affinity to his soul. There is some peace, despite all the physical weakness that is there. The big body is unstable and tipsy. He quietly gives thanks to God and to Kuan Yin for their help. Something has happened to him during his illness which now brings clarity to his mind.

He sits there for a long quiet time. Even in the absence of sun the temple seems to glow. He does not ask for anything. He apparently has enough, enough at least to start. So, in time, he goes out the front of the temple. There is a freshness in the air. He thinks he will go see his people. This time he wears his robe which he has never worn away from the temple. He excuses himself by saying that he is not going to do any physical work, and he needs protection because he is not strong. He walks lightly and proudly, but not too steadily, to the first house across from the temple.

He goes inside where he is greeted with warmth. They have not seen him for a long time. They ask him where he has been, and he answers that he has been on a long trip to learn so that he can help them. He brings all of the household people together, the sick and the weak. He remembers how very healthy these people were when he first came. Now they are very poorly looking and no one is well. He tells them that now is the time for them to heal themselves. They start to complain, saying that this is impossible, that there is no feeling, that they are too old or weak or that they are too ill. He tells them that they are still alive and are closer to their soul than before and this soul is divine. He tells them that there is a power on earth also which they call God, which is overwhelmingly beautiful, true, correct, brilliant and it is a part of all people, to be shared with all things. This is what divine means; they are to command the world in its growth, in its repair from illness and in its evolution. The people have forgotten this. He tells them that when man forgets his divine greatness, he is subjected to the chaos which overwhelms the beauty of the nature of life. Those who are still alive are the strongest and most gifted. They are to move on and rise above the disease and the illness that has come upon their bodies. He says that as this occurs, the rains will return to the land and the animals will bring forth new animals.

He asks each one to go with him to find that place within themselves that he has spoken of and to know its truth. He moves from household to household with the same message. It is a firm message and it is a "self" message. At every household they say, "Yes, but we cannot, look at what has happened to our land. Look what has happened to our bodies. Look at what has happened to our cattle." And he says, "It will all return. People are healed when they allow divine information to come to them and to incorporate it into their lives. They may see such healing as a miracle. It is not easily explained until they feel the purity and strength of divine power...a power which causes their bodies to be endowed with health that does not participate with disease causing situations." Naibhu said, "What happens in plagues is the "will" of the people has become dormant. They find their passive natures so essential for body recovery. Unfortunately, passivity can damper the "will" which directs the soul's energy to live and prosper. You are the healer of yourself if you find your divine essence. If you can find your divine place, it will be more abundant than you have ever known." With each little group that he goes to, he shows radiant strength, more than they have ever seen in him. When he leaves he sits awhile and wonders what is happening to him, and he weeps.

He stops occasionally to be with the animals to tell them that the terrible cycle is nearly ending, that they will feel the urge of life and they will breed and bring forth multiple, multiple animals. They will be strengthened when they see that only the strong remain.

The little children come and sit on his lap. They touch his face and they hear. They hear so simply and so easily. He tells them that they have special, special work to do, that when the older people doubt, they are to allow this beauty to shine, to touch them and to comfort them because they know. He is given some meager food which he does not feel that he needs, but people want to share what little they have left. Each day as his people grow stronger, they glean the fields and they find grain to eat.

As the sun is setting on that day, Naibhu has brought

his first great message, one that he truly knows. He moves slowly back toward his temple, and as he goes up the steps he realizes that this is his first day as a spiritual leader of people. He weeps again...without total comprehension, but he knows that he is changing.

Inside his temple he gives thanks for his people and for their life and recovery. The temple is lit by some great light. He sees the Kuan Yin and he feels her hand upon his head as she says, "Now you are ready to be taught. Your knowing will come in great abundance and your physical vitality will return. You will find your spiritual strength. You have told the people today why you came. It was not to rebuild their temple, but it was to help them rebuild their lives and to find the divine part of their being."

He hears magnificent music and he sees. He sees the temple full of people. He knows that they will come. They will not come to find; they will come to share, to be together in the new life that they are building. The temples are a place not to find something but to share something. He sees the little ones...the little ones are the great teachers. He sees them going to people whose strength is not quite there. With those who falter, the little ones climb into their laps and touch them. He has some apostles. They are called children.

Naibhu has great happiness. He sees the people coming to the temple to give thanks and to share. He does not go to his bed that night. He stays in the temple where the light surrounds and holds him in a spiritual reverie...it strengthens and nourishes him.

The morning comes; he is still sitting where he was when the sun went down. This morning he is even more refreshed, for he has slept the highest sleep for a long, long time. He goes out again to see his people, to make the long trek to every home. This time he is greeted by the little children first. They know he will come. They run out to hold his hand and to take him in. They need to show him that the people are a little better. When he enters, their faces look like there is still doubt, and they say a lot of "yes, buts" to him. He reminds them, "You heard me yesterday. You heard what I said. I have the same message today, only today it is stronger and so are you!" His mind is as clear as it was yesterday. He tells them that he sees their awareness is back, looking more substantial. He expects they will heal rapidly and that the rains will come soon. He adds that the temple is open to them.

Each place he goes there is a new glimmer of hope that has been in suppression. That hope comes back and goes, but it stays long enough for them to realize that they are to change their way of thinking. He does not answer the questions they ask him. He radiates and he talks about the divine. Some cling to their weaknesses, telling him that they cannot plant. They are much too weak to work. He laughs with them, insisting that what he is talking about has absolutely no weakness. God's energy is total strength and has no limitations. He tells them that they are to think of what they want to do first and not what they cannot do. He refuses to listen to their excuses. He stays long enough that they stop their excuses also. They beg him to return tomorrow. He tells them that as long as they need him, he will be there. His is a message of hope, a message of strength and a message of love. He tells each one of them that when they weaken, when they doubt, they are to call a little child to help them, and as they help little children to learn and to grow, the little child will help them with their divinity.

Everywhere he goes, the children meet him and when he leaves, the children follow until he sends them back. They are truly escorting him, making him joyful. They have become such happy little ones, still weak but glowing. Their hope is more and greater than anyone else's hope.

The rains come. They are gentle and not the deluge rains of most years. Every day the rains continue. A little at first then a little more. The monsoons are more docile this year. He shares joy with the people that life will come anew to the land. He tells them in their eagerness to come back to health that they are never to forget what they have brought with them this time, what has sustained them, what they really are and how precious it is for the world. With the abundance which would come into their life, they are to give praise for this. Always. Foremost.

Chapter Twenty-Nine

Naibhu sits in the little temple and he wonders why his heart is so heavy, for he has everything he needs or has ever wanted. He has people, who are very kind. He has flowers for his Kuan Yin. He has plenty of food but he has the feeling of impending danger. The things that have become important in his life have changed. There is happiness but there is also a sadness. He is with his people, yet he is not with his people.

He goes out for a walk. He sits down a minute to see the countryside that has recovered from the drought. The hills are green and the crops are abundant, the animals are flourishing and the people are healthy. The people have picked up the pieces. Everything is beautiful and ideal except that he is troubled. When things are difficult, he does not feel troubled. He asks Kuan Yin what is happening to him. "You are around the flowers, the trees and the people," she says, "but where is God?" Naibhu asks why God seems to trouble him; he complains that when God is with him he experiences so much power that he shakes. In the days that follow, he experiences great heat and he sits in meditation. The temple seems particularly rosy with vitalizing red glows. With this energy he moves farther out into the countryside visiting people and carrying his message. Naibhu has spiritual feelings but he has more. He has determination also, for the white and silver clouds that surround him are stronger with more power than ever. He senses that this radiance carries his message and the power makes it stick. Even the doubters follow. He is supposed to rally the doubters not the followers. His leadership is stronger. The temple flourishes. People come from long distances to participate in the very special energies and the love they experience in the temple. Naibhu tries to teach the people that the love of God can only be found within themselves. They do not have to go any place but within themselves to find that very, very special energy of God. And as they change their thinking, they will know God. The vases are always full of flowers for the Kuan Yins.

Around the village there are lots of new baby goats. As he walks along the paths to greet his people, he puts a goat under each arm. When the people come daily into the temple, Naibhu can no longer deny his leadership. He takes more responsibility and guides his people without hesitation or worry. Yet, his role is not totally satisfactory to him. Things are accomplished for others but not completely for him. He has unfinished business.

One day he starts out of the little village on his work not knowing where he is going, but he is angry and annoyed. He has something personally to do with himself and he cannot be about it or find it. He is fiddling around. As he nears the outskirts of the village, he turns back abruptly. He wants a baby goat to go with him up into the hills. When a person hesitates to loan him a little one, he assures them that he will return it safely in a few days. He just needs a goat companion on a trip he has to make. He picks out a particularly appealing one with all over color spots like Juda and sticks it under his arm as he starts out of town again.

He looks into the hills, seeing a particularly lovely spot overlooking this valley. The gently rolling land has some trees. Back into his memory comes the Buddhic temple where he had been angered by the temple trappery. Now he takes his goat and again heads for the hills. He thinks he will just sit there until something happens. He will fast and be with this goat, and there he will stay, doing nothing, until something happens. He is miserable, upset and frustrated, and there does not seem to be anything to change his moods. He is not going to do anything until something happens. He is upset. He is frustrated. There does not seem to be any way to change it.

On the way he has time to be very infuriated. He is annoyed and he is stubborn. He mumbles to himself saying, "I guess I am supposed to be here to get taught. If it comes, it better be an important teaching or I will not participate."

He is bewildered and most of all sick of waiting. He says if something is going to happen, let's have it now. Then he thinks he hears a voice questioning, "Are you ready for it?" Naibhu thinks, "I do not know but I think so. Bring it to me and I will tell you." He continues to experience anger because nothing is happening. He says enough is enough. He recognizes that he is impatient, annoyed and miserable. He wants to quit, not knowing what it means to quit.

The little goat yells for its mother. It wants to go back to the goat farm. Naibhu thinks that the goat is of no help. A couple of sad beings up on the hill. He looks at the little critter and he picks it up and strokes it, as he talks to it. He remembers when he was a tiny little boy what the goats had done for him. He continues with that silly little animal, curled up in his arm, thinking, "How did I get here anyway?" It seems he always follows some direction wherever he goes. When he gets there he is supposed to go somewhere else so he just goes. He wonders when he is going to find something that he wants to do. He thinks about that idea for a little while. He does not know what he wants to do, so he guesses it is just as well to be sent by someone else, someone that knows what he is supposed to do, because he does not know. He is a very miserable man. He no longer wants to follow the caravans. He could care less. But he has no substitute he really cares about. The temple is all done. People are in the temple. Maybe he will just take off and be a continuous wanderer...that would be better, work a day here and a day there, get his food and then move on. That would be good. He tries everything he knows to escape. Something weighs heavily on his head.

His goat gets hungry; he must feed the little critter, so he goes to find something. He thinks that the goat is a mistake. He hears the birds and he is not interested. He sees the flowers and he forgets them. He gets hungry and he is not motivated. To hell with his hunger. He is not satisfied with what he is going to do. He is not going to do a thing about it! He does go find the little goat something to eat though. It eats happily as he watches. Stupid animal! Eating makes it happy while he is miserable and nothing works. He tries to remember if he has ever been so miserable and he does not think so. He remembers outside the big town when he had been confused, but this time he is miserable. He is not interested in anything and he does not like being here. Furthermore, he refuses to give in to his appetite. If the thought comes to hustle something to eat, he eliminates it. His stomach will growl, but he is not going to feed it. And he is not going to return to the village either. He is not going to get himself busy either. He is going to stay on in these strange hills until something happens. He looks toward the people in that village. There is action going on and he is glad they can straighten themselves out. The little goat cuddles up to him and he holds it. He asks for the Kuan Yin, but she does not come.

He wants to sleep but is too miserable. He wants to return to his sickness and he wants to go back where there is nothing. That is where he wants to go...back there to nothing. He would just as soon quit. He does not know whether he wants to continue this kind of life. His is most unsatisfactory. Ah ha! He has remembered something. He is remembering the last time he went up the mountain with Juda. They had a glorious time together playing and romping and being carefree. He remembers how he got in touch with his spirit. It was very profound. He came down carefree and happy then with something calling him to the people by the river. He remembers going down to that river with Juda who had gone to the little boy that drowned. He remembers the little girl who came and grabbed him by the leg. He sees himself putting his hand on the little boy's head just as he had with goats when they died. Most of all he remembers his shock after bringing the little boy back to life. He recalls how these people looked at him like he was someone else. He was afraid of the power that came through him. He tried not to comprehend what is happening, yet he knows well that the little boy lives! He asks God to please go do his miracles but not involve him.

He cannot fully understand why this soul had such a tremendously difficult time. He wants to call it quits. The only thing he can figure out...he is afraid of the overwhelming power that now seems to be coming into his soul. It has no barriers. If he could only just watch it happen from the outside, he would not object. But it has to be in him, through him, by him and with him. He asks for more time to slow up the energies coming to him so that he can make some adjustments. He gets a powerful message, "Your time is up. There is no more time; this is it!" He is told that he has come to the hills to receive the great gift that he will now give to mankind and is he ready for the gift? His answer is that he is not ready; he will not lead.

He is not sleeping. He is not resting. He is not eating.

He calls the Kuan Yin and she comes. She touches him and tells him that the problem is within him but she will give him support. He asks complainingly why it should be so difficult. She responds that the struggle will only strengthen his gift. She reminds him to be patient, that his life has been incredibly difficult. She repeats that the struggles that have taken place for him to live would have overcome most people. Now he has to come to his primary struggle for the recognition and manifestation of his divine power. He too knows that to live is not enough, no matter how much he dislikes this new path.

Each time as he recognizes his spiritual power and when he understands it, tears come to his eyes. Although he knows he is destined to move completely into the spiritual level, only part of him is there. The other part stays quite separate. Again he recognizes the tenacity of his personality which is help and hindrance. But Naibhu has taken another step; he no longer wishes to be as he was; his life will be more complete. Out in the hills, Naibhu is stirring. Energy flicks from him to the world and back again replenishing him. His body is stiff but energized. The little goat who has been helpful now wants his mother. Naibhu holds and cuddles him. Strange that such a hard little head contains such limpid, sweet big eyes. Down the hill he starts, back to the village to be about his ministry.

The village is bustling with activity. It has been some days since he has been there. The people greet him warmly; they have missed him. He returns the goat with a special loving pat. It is a new day and time for him.

Chapter Thirty

Naibhu stands very tall this day. He walks along as though he has overcome his problem. He sees the people. They come around and he touches them. They want him to stay, but he declines; he has to be about his mission and as he moves on he feels very joyful. Some peace has returned to him. He moves on down the road.

People along the roads with the carts offer him rides. He chooses to walk instead. At another village people bring many babies for his blessing. He has never blessed a baby; he has only held a few before and he feels clumsy. They believe his blessing will somehow protect this child, but he does not know about blessing. He does not say anything; he just holds and smiles at them. They coo and everyone enjoys that. There are many babies for him to learn from. People are smiling. There are some old people who come to him and ask him to bless them. They feel refreshed. Although people ask for his blessing, he never remembers having blessed them. It seems easy. He talks to them. The ones that feel afraid are eased when he talks to them. They seem to know where he comes from and why he came, as though a messenger has told them of his coming. Slowly from nowhere a brief glimmer of understanding about a "blessing" came into his thoughts. He remembers how he treated little animals that had died. He put his fingers over their eyes and asked for their divine existence. Was this what people called a "blessing" for the living?

At the road junction he is guided to turn west into a narrow, mostly unused road going toward the hills and less fertile land. He sees no one on the road but imagines it goes somewhere. Anyway, he likes the solitude. At times he senses things are not good, but he continues. Around a corner he sees a small group of houses that look abandoned; he wonders why the people left, hoping they have moved to better soil. The road ends abruptly just past the last house with a small circle turn around. Naibhu becomes curious. Nothing moves, no people, no animals and no carts. Yet, he senses that there are people there inside those buildings and behind the barred windows and doors. He calls out at each door but gets no answer. With some frustration he has the urge to kick in a door and ease his curiosity. But he is wearing his robe and the priestly feelings do not allow him to be violent. As is his custom when things are not clear, he keeps a vigil under a tree to commune with his higher friends.

He waits a whole day, sensing he is being watched but without visible signs. He feels perserverating anger and frustration, so unexpressed. As Naibhu guides people, these feelings are not new to him, but generally he works with one-sided anger. Anger at an absent person is somehow less intense than what is in this village. Here is mutual, smoldering and direct anger. He knows that whatever is going on has been happening for some time and now is at a climax. This is why he has been called to this village. He senses that here he will learn a great lesson of confrontation. Late in the afternoon a few small domestic animals appear and approach Naibhu curiously. As though a switch has been activated, Naibhu radiates. It seems that the more cautious these animals become the more glowing his body becomes. Few can resist the attraction. Naibhu wonders at this strange behavior. He always loves animals and they in turn accept him easily. But none before had crawled to him to touch him gently and to lie docile around him. He wonders why without an answer. Although Naibhu had only been aware of common night noises, most of these animals do not leave him throughout the night.

In the morning he senses shadows pass windows...an awakening inside. A small figure appears from behind the house—a young boy calls to his dog. The dog acknowledges his friend but does not go to him. Ever so slowly he approaches Naibhu. It is obvious someone has given him permission to find out about the big priest in the brown robe who attracts their pets.

Naibhu calls out to him saying he has been awaiting him and he has been sent to this village to be of help if something has happened. The child looks back to his house several times before sitting beside Naibhu. He is both reluctant and eager to talk—to unburden his mind. Soon he knows Naibhu can help. He confides how sad everyone is—that something has befallen their village—some evil spirit has caused a loss of crops at one house, animals to become sick at another, a new baby to be born crippled at a third and the patriarch who keeps feelings evenly anchored has died at the last house.

Naibhu cannot understand why people have withdrawn from the world because of these losses. He asks the child where his playmates are, only to learn that families do not talk to families and children are not allowed to play with other children. Naibhu is confused because all the child can tell him is that different people in those houses made these things happen. And with this the child picks up his dog and scampers behind a house. Naibhu does not understand the problem, but he has long since learned not to try to solve the problem at the level of the problem. It never works; for the problem is always that the people's personal problems color each situation. He does not stay in the village that night; he goes beyond the road into the rocks where inspiration always comes easily. He calls his beautiful Kuan Yin but the ancient old man and many others come with her. He wonders if the Ancient One would teach the same truths as the "beautiful lady." He asks why did he need him. He is answered quickly by the man saying there is no difference in the wisdom of their teaching, but with material problems requiring judgments concerning people, Naibhu needed both the male and female perspectives to understand and give the wisest help. And in the hush of the night darkness, his other senses sleep while he is taught. To ease his curiosity, he is told that the old Patriarch who has died had held these four family groups under his will for many years. They are all closely related and they looked to him with ultimate dependency. He had always been a cruel, uncompromising man who ruled by first encouraging rivalry and jealousy within houses and families. In the last years his influence started to wane, causing him to predict disasters and attribute losses to some kind of a curse one family places upon another. Existing tensions were fanned as events took place to confirm his prediction.

Old angers flared and new happenings fueled them. No one wished to change. Abruptly, this information stops, Naibhu wants and needs no more—the real problem becomes clear to him. All of these people have lost the capacity to "love." Naibhu becomes uneasy since he has never thought too much about love, except that most of his life he had not trusted people enough to love them. And then when he discovered his "beautiful lady," he had intense times of love, but not always and not every time he saw her. Sometimes she annoyed him and created problems. Then when he found God, he experienced love—a lot. But he never much thought about it. Now he knows he needs to be very wise about love for these people are very experienced in non-love.

He has found the correct question, "Tell me about love, so I may know and serve these people." As with all humans who clearly pose the problem, whose motivations are direct and clear, the answers come readily to Naibhu. He never knows from whence the answers come, but throughout the night he learns, knowing that these teachings are divinely inspired. This is what he learns.

"Love is a deeply emotional state that is rarely rational and often blind. It is encumbered with childhood memories. Love, a feeling, is experienced by infants when their needs and wants are met, giving them pleasure. Because of the long dependency of children these needs are constantly satisfied by others and they learn that these feelings are called, 'love'. Thus the child believes that love is by another person. Love then becomes attached to a person and later to an object. Children love their doll or an animal because these satisfy a need and give them pleasure.

"Further, love experiences are confused when humans, knowing how powerful love needs are, barter love by giving and taking it away as punishment or praise. Love becomes 'out there', requiring another person. As time goes on people become possessive of 'love objects' and 'loved ones' and will not share. People then become prisoners of these beliefs; they entrap themselves. By so doing they lose the greatest human gift that God has given, the capacity for 'lovingness'. The thought that before one can truly love another, one must first love one's self does not clarify the feeling. For love that is still attached to any object like 'me' is also not free."

"Better that humans describe their feelings as 'lovingness' a state of being, God given, that allows each to radiate joy and life and warmth, his divineness, available to all humans and living things which wish to tap into it. 'Lovingness' is not directed toward anything. No permission is necessary to partake of it and nothing is requested in return. In 'lovingness' there is no hidden purpose save the sheer exuberance of being. This truly is unconditional love."

Naibhu cherishes these thoughts throughout the night and in the day he knows these are so deep within his mind he can never forget. He wonders, however, how these profound thoughts could be used with these people so bound in their mystical fears and worldly wants. Slowly he retraces his steps to a waiting place under the trees. He knows the time and opportunity will be presented and he will know and act.

As usual no one stirs. He hears some little people's voices behind houses and little faces peer around them. Naibhu remembers his Apostles, the little children and how they had heard his message of "self help" during the plague. He had the answer. Little children will open the hearts of their families and he knows how. Naibhu tones, softly and gently, as though the sounds come from far away over the hills, coming closer and closer beckoning to the children. And as the sound moves so do they. They come from everywhere to the end of the road and they circle the trees. Each is acknowledged and each settles nearby to begin his toning. And as they tone they radiate and as they radiate they release the burdens that they carry, burdens they accepted from their families that were not really theirs. They begin to play again like children. When energies are expended, Naibhu calls them to him to thank them for the wonderful day of joy. He asks each to think and remember how he feels and to lock in that feeling forever so he will take it back to his home to share with all. He tells the children that when adults are heavy and sorrowful they are to come near them and share their feeling. And if family tries to discourage their "lovingness" they must tell them that God has sent the nice priest to ease their sorrow, as he did theirs. The little ones are indeed Naibhu's "miracle workers." Each day they come and tone and play around him and each day he notices more signs of normalcy around houses. Some adults come to question him and they stay to learn. Eventually most come, not relating to each other but to him and their joy as children. Naibhu tells them of his learning on the night when he was taught about "love" and "lovingness." He shares these mysteries as he shares his "lovingness," his radiance. Before he leaves, he knows that the seeds of change are planted deeply. His work is over and he moves on.

He moves on down to a valley where men are felling trees. They call out to him; they want him to see a man who has been injured. Naibhu looks at them as they motion for him to heal the man. Naibhu is afraid but he puts his hands over the man's injury and the wound heals rapidly. Naibhu sits on a log and ponders about healing. He has never tried to heal an injury before. The workers swarm around him. He has a sudden urge to go back to his temple, but he knows he still has much to learn. He is happy enough despite the fact that he does not know where he is going. He just moves on. There is something about him which is very peaceful.

He moves along down the road into another valley. Again, the people come to him and they sit around asking him questions. Most of the questions have to do with things that Naibhu does not know so he does not talk very much. He just sits there radiant saying very few words. He seems to be teaching people in his own way. His teaching is manifesting. He is not teaching by trying to convince. He is teaching by being. He does not quite understand what is happening, but he knows it is new and he must teach this way. He just sits there amongst them and this is apparently what they need. Very sad people come and go away feeling better. He does nothing and yet they feel better. He does not lay on hands and yet they improve.

Wherever he goes, it is always the same. If he lingers by the fields, the people stop to come to him. He is aware that his path takes a large circle to the north and east of his own temple. He will not return to his temple until he has completed the full circle. He proceeds down to the foot of the valley where the orchards are. There are people working around the trees. As he moves amongst them they stop their work and sit with him. He shares his experiences with the people, the experiences of discovering God. He tells them that they too can experience God if they decide to do so. He says he is just learning how to do it and that he has been sent on this mission to find out. He insists that every man can experience God fully but it is each person's responsibility—no one can make him experience God in himself. He has come along on this trip in order to learn and tell the people how to experience God. He tells them that whenever they have a problem, they must experience God first. After they have experienced God, then they will have the solution to their problem. He moves on. The people do not want him to go, but he is called to complete his journey and he moves on.

His work is the same for many days. People seek him, asking him questions, with different needs...needs he sees as ultimately the same. They needed to know and to grasp for themselves that they are God manifest. It is a very quiet time in Naibhu's life. He is not too sure about what is happening to him as he moves along to the people with his radiant message. He senses that apparently they have been waiting for him, the "Awaited One." He heals and blesses and comforts the sick and disturbed. But most of all he carries a very simple message. He carries only one message to all people and to teach this thing he needs to be it.

He sees another temple, a large and older temple than his. From a distance he knows that it is a place where he does not wish to go! Yet, compulsively he is drawn to it. First he stands off to one side watching the many people going in an out. Naibhu notes that they appear agitated as though they are angry. There are numerous people sitting or lying on the sides of the long steps entering the temple. Most are children. All of them are sick, maimed or crippled with obvious handicaps. He has never seen so many unwhole children. As people pass these children who are on side steps, they do not look at them. Instead, they hasten their walking and keep on going. In fact, he wonders if they see them at all. Everyone hurries by the children. Some throw things at them without looking, coins and bits of food. But still they are not acknowledged, as though they do not exist. People's facial expressions never change when they approach the children.

Naibhu sits down on the steps where the children are. He is so large, he fears that he might frighten them. He faces a serious dilemma about what to do with these children, and it becomes his major concern as if they all belong to him. He has never seen so many little beggars in one place, each with his hand out, each with a pleading face. He wants so much to help each child, to remove his pain and make him well but all he knows is to bless each one. The Kuan Yin appears beside him. Slowly he embraces each child, poor little waifs that they are. Naibhu has never felt more love or spirit. As he ministers his kind of Godliness, the children begin to change; dramatically they change. He sees some of them stand and walk, others move crippled limbs. Not only do the bones and muscles work but the scars and inhuman appearances of their bodies seem to melt away. They become for a brief time like normal, healthy children. He cannot believe what he sees. He tries to deny the thought of what is happening for he does not believe what he sees. He remains on the steps for some time where both he and the children are in another state of consciousness. He stays there trying to comprehend the miracle that is happening. When he moves from a state of ecstasy, he feels a stirring to go into the temple. The little ones follow him.

The thought comes that there is a monster in the temple. As he enters the door, he becomes suddenly very ill. What he sees is great, big ugly things, grotesque statues, desperate serpents. And directly in front is one ugly, old Buddha. He has never seen such a diabolical face and fat, ugly body. In a flash he grabs it with his big hands, lifting it from its seat. Raising it over his head, he dashes it to the floor in a thousand pieces. Then he stamps upon what is left and spits upon it. The people see him do it; they leave quickly. Angrily he pulls down the flags and heavy material, leaving it in a pile on the top of the Buddha pieces. He does not know how in an instant his "loving," divine state changes to violence and destruction. He had experienced that level of rage before but only when his life was threatened and never, never such a sudden reversal. Then he rushes outside to be with the children. He is very angry and confused. He does not know exactly why he has made a shambles out of everything but somehow he is glad. He has made a statement which he needs to make. He has rejected the decadence that has distorted the most beautiful thing he knows, a chance to praise the "divine spirit" by creating beautiful things.

He is surrounded by the children's excited faces and moving bodies. He is very angry. He looks at the people drawing back from him as if they are afraid...all except the little ones who squeeze closer and closer around him. They will not leave him. The people look at the children in awe. Now that the children are so improved, they no longer want them. They are not good beggars anymore. People slither down the stairs and are gone.

This is a horrible, horrible temple that Naibhu wants to totally destroy. He goes back into the temple with that in mind. When he sees what he has done to punish distorted minds, he knows that he should do better. The viciousness has left him. He comes to realize that the children are now his children. He bows his head. There is nothing else in his life that he is totally responsible for. Children?

He believes that he cannot take the children back to their homes and leave them. He does not want to return the children to parents who have maimed them and sent them to beg. He sits down on the temple steps with these children whose little bodies seem less distorted. He knows that they understand. All night he remains with these little ones on the steps. It is as though his arms are big enough to surround each one of them, to cover them, to protect them; like a giant cloak of velvet, he wraps around them and he sits there until the day arrives. He has accepted the greatest responsibility of his life—bodies to feed, to protect and hardest of all, children to teach to love humans again and to show them that their souls are a part of God.

Chapter Thirty-One

Still on the temple steps in the early morning, Naibhu, with his great arms wrapped around his little brood, has covered many with his great cloak. They have been at peace all night while he has been in wonderment. He wonders about the power of God that he has seen manifested in the healing of little children. Hardly able to comprehend what has happened, yet knowing it is a divine order that these are to be his children to care for.

As the sun comes up, local people start back into the temple. He sees strange people, accompanied by a very, very old priest, crippled and full of sorrow. As the priest enters into the temple, a long distance away from Naibhu...completely on the other side of the steps, fearful people were with him. They go inside this strange temple painted all over the outside with ugly red snakes and serpents with wild eyes. They do not come near Naibhu.

As though they are afraid of him, they move to the other side of the entrance. Somehow, he wants to get away from that temple before he destroys it all. His heart is singing and he does not wish to go back inside again to see the ugliness, the sadness of the people who are there and to know what has happened to him.

He tells the children he must take them to their own homes. He knows that they do not want to go, yet he knows also that he has to try to return them to their families. The children know that they are starting a new life, never to go back. So it is a token act when he leads the twelve or thirteen children back into the small village where he has not yet been. He goes to each child's house to deliver him back into that poverty. But the parents will not accept them into their homes. They bar the doors. They curse at him through the windows and they tell him to go away and take the children. They do not want them. Some deny that these are their children. Naibhu knows that truly they belong to no human, they belong to God and he, Naibhu, is to be their custodian.

As they move through the village, the children become happier and happier. It as though a tremendous party is taking place. When they reach the edge of the village he has all the children. They went to each place to return a little being to where he lives and at each place he has been rejected. Naibhu heads away from the village to the countryside that he loves so well, knowing this time he will not stop. He is going around, completing the circle back to his temple with his little ones. There is much joy as he moves along. He knows the little ones are hungry yet he has no food. When he gets outside of the village, he stops by a farmer's to ask if he can spare just a little food so he can feed his children. He says that he is taking them to a place where they will be very happy, that he has found them in poverty. A lot of them are emaciated but somehow full of energy on this day. Each place he stops he is given more food. The littlest ones get the food first. Somehow it feeds everyone.

Naibhu's heart is very, very joyful. His spirit soars

and his blanket of love goes around each child. They are totally protected. They tone. They tone the kind of toning that Naibhu has occasionally heard. It is little people's toning...little people's sounds. It is faint, sweet and the most lyrical music he has ever heard. Instantaneously happy, little people smile back at him.

At night they rest. It takes two days to get to his temple—two days and a part of a next day. As he comes into the village, he wonders how long he has been gone. It is more than a few days, more like a few weeks. But his temple is still there. The people come out in wonderment at Naibhu who comes leading his little ones. He tells them where he has found them, that God has cured them and that their people refused to accept them. Now everyone has a responsibility to care for these little ones.

The days that follow are the most fulfilling days of Naibhu's life. He knows nothing about little children, yet he knows everything about them. As he teaches them, he finds a tenderness that he has glimpsed occasionally in his life, but not as tenderly as now.

His every waking minute is to make sure that every single moment of their new life is full of joy and of love. He keeps them first inside the temple. A few days later he finds an old barn like building full of soft hay and straw where they can sleep more comfortably. It is cozy and smells good. He sleeps in the barn with them, to ease their fears.

Each day the people come to get the little children to work with them. He is very careful that the tiny ones do not work very long, but they should work—they need to, but they should also play. The older ones can work longer. These people need this work in the community where there are not many young ones. Every day he takes each child where he is to go, sees what he is to do and that it is not too heavy and too hard for him because God had entrusted him as the custodian for the group. It is the most important work he has ever done. They are fed and they are free. They are working their way, each in his own small way.

Early morning they come to the temple to be with Naibhu. He sits with them inside the temple and they tone. They are so happy and so is he. He teaches them about love, about joy and about life. He teaches them all the things that he had never known when he was a little boy. Some kind of sense is there, but he never quite has time to find it. These little ones have time and he is their teacher.

Out behind the temple, down the hill they start growing their own vegetables. The soil is not good but everything grows beautifully, magnificently, from such rocky soil. The small ones are taught to plant and to love the soil. The littlest ones play around; they want to be with the others. They are too tiny to do much work except carry a few rocks or a little bowl of water. Everything the children touch grows and grows. Before the soil had seemed so barren and poor that it was worthless.

He teaches them about goats. The oldest boys take care of goats that are right behind the temple. Each morning the goats follow the children down the hill to the gardens. What a glorious time this is for Naibhu! It is as though all the pain in his life has gone. Each day is long and full. The little ones seem to be thriving; the older ones care for the younger ones and Naibhu's work becomes less and less.

New people start coming into his temple from some distance. People he has not known before he took that long trip around the community. They come from separate villages when they hear where he is. They come from that village where he has talked to them about love and the fighting has stopped. They bring him a magnificent new robe. It is green and gold and the women have made it by hand. It is almost too beautiful for him. He has his old brown one that is all full of tatters, all worn but now he has a beautiful new bright green robe! He puts it in his little room. He does not know quite what to do with it...it seems almost too beautiful.

The people keep coming and coming. Each day when he finishes with his children and as they are about their work or their play, Naibhu goes back to the temple steps to meet his people. They are coming from everywhere. He is amazed. They come and they come. He knows that they come only with troubles. They bring the sick and the old, the infirmed and the sorrowful. Each day the roads are full of people who come to the temple. Each day he shows them life. He shows them the life of young people at work and at play and he shows them joy and happiness. He asks them to tell him about their problems, yet he only half listens because Naibhu knows that what they tell him is not the problem.

His temple steps are filled. He talks to groups about the same thing. He tells them that God will fill their life if they can experience what the spirit of God means to them. Sometimes they are angry with him because they want something else and he does not listen. He only says they have come a long ways and he has a message. When they listen, he talks very little. The power and divine radiance that comes through him cannot be denied. The people change as he teaches them to remember the experiences they are having. He tells them that they already know everything, and they have only forgotten it.

He encourages them to remember. He tells them if they follow this highest knowing they will have a life of love, beauty and plenty. And they do. He tells them to come into the temple and give praise to God, for there is no problem that cannot be solved. If their problems are still there, these burdens should be left outside for as they cross the threshold inside the temple, there is to be peace and joy. There they would sing God's praises.

Each day they come to hear again and learn the same message. It is a message to the people to heal themselves and to love life. Naibhu knows that he never really healed anyone, but he also knows that when they come to him, they find faith. Each person that comes takes faith back with him. He tells them whatever they have found and experienced there, they are to teach to all people, to others with troubles and problems. They are to remember the joy of God in everyone and to experience it. Each day Naibhu goes to bed a fulfilled man, joyful, full of wonderment.

Each day it is the same again. He puts on his green robe when he has finished with the chores and the children are fed. The children are happy. With good food, they grow healthy and loving. They come in the morning to tone with him. It is a glorious time in the temple. The joy of love is all consuming.

Each day people come anew and he knows not from whence they come and he does not care. Mostly they are not free; they come in sadness and they leave in love. Naibhu still insists that no one should enter the temple except with love. If there is anything but joy within them, they must stand on the steps of the temple for that is where these problems will be coped with.

One day several townspeople come from a little village where he has blessed the babies. The people come to bring him another robe; it is purple and gold! He keeps it inside the temple saying that he will not wear it outside. Every day when he meets with the people and the children inside the temple, he puts on his purple robe. When he meets them on the steps, he wears his green one. The tattered brown robe he saves to work in the gardens and the fields. He now has three robes. He has a farm robe; he has an outside robe; and he has an inside robe. He has many possessions!

Sometimes at night when Naibhu falls exhausted into his bed he wonders and talks with the Kuan Yin. Often he talks to God and he says, "It is like a miracle that I can hardly understand." He is part of it; he sees it, but it is somehow difficult for his humanness to understand. What has happened to the children, his love for the people and for growing things—all miracles! Each day, early in the morning, he goes to stand on the temple steps where he stays all day, meeting the people and listening. Sometimes he tells them about his life, his discoveries and how hard it has been to change and accept the gifts that God made available. He lets them know that he is human like they are. The greatest problem of humans, he tells them, is to be both human and divine, simultaneously.

This is his and their unfinished business, the reason for their lives. Each time they catch a glimpse of the divine light, they leave the temple with their eyes shining. He encourages them to bring that joy, that love and that spirit to everyone around them because the love in their lives is God. They do as he bids them and bring other people to the temple.

Naibhu seems to be toning all of the time. He never stops toning. He tones when he walks. He tones with people that come to share with him their joys. He is firm in his teaching: "Do not take your problems into the temple. Stay on the steps with your problems." It does not make any difference whether they go into the temple. By afternoon the temple has spread, filling the front and the back lawns.

Each morning he watches the little ones come and go to their chores. He often sits down on the steps and talks to them about growing things and about animals. But he also talks about knowing God and about beauty. Naibhu is so glad, at times it is as though his heart would burst. The people are feeding him with their love, and he knows that they are giving him more than he can possibly give them. No wonder he is very glad.

Chapter Thirty-Two

Naibhu is with a group of people in one corner of the temple. He has on his purple and gold robe. The radiant light around him is gold. Each morning of every day he meets the early ones and stays until the last person has left. People who come now are different; they are younger and less troubled. Those who came in the beginning, came to gain help. Now they come giving... giving... giving. They bring food for the children and others in need. They bring money. Naibhu takes very little money, only enough for the needs of the children. The children do not need much money because most things are bartered. They also bring clothes for the older children and play things for the little ones. Naibhu has no personal need for any money. There are plenty of supplies. What they do not use of the gifts, he gives to the poor. Life is very simple and it just seems to roll on without problems.

People bring their little ones to be blessed and he blesses them. They come to be married and he leads them as they marry themselves. He tells them that he knows no ritual but God does and will marry them. He takes care of them all and counsels them wisely.

Naibhu thinks that his abundance is profound. Nothing else has happened to him. He has people who love him. He has opportunities to serve. He has little ones to bring joy. He has growing things and living animals. He has the glory of the Kuan Yin.

He is sharing each morning with the little ones as they come to start their day. The temple faces east and the light that comes into the arches sends each away with a singing heart. At night when all is done and his people have left, Naibhu goes back into his beautiful temple and sits between the two Kuan Yins. He remembers the Kuan Yin that had first come to him as a small boy and had taken him to the goats that cared for him. He knows it is the power of the Kuan Yin that has saved his life many times and that gives him something he cannot describe. He remembers how he had lost touch with Kuan Yin until he had found the people and Juda; now that he is a leader in the community, she comes to his awareness and gives him strength. When he was confused and lost in the big city and sat up in the rocks sobbing, the Kuan Yin came to him that time and he had visions. She held him and she led him to this temple where he found her statues.

Each night he gives thanks to the "beautiful lady." One night she speaks to him and says that all is well around him, but he has another lesson to learn. Naibhu thinks his life is so full that he does not need more lessons. He cannot quite understand what she is trying to tell him when she says that there are great spirits to communicate with him to give him information that he does not have. Naibhu does not quite understand. She assures him that there are others like her in spirit form who have great wisdom who will teach him to tap into all information. He does not have to know everything if he can contact information sources. He does not have to know. He is very puzzled. No one had really ever taught Naibhu. He had learned everything from his experiences. No one had ever taken the time to teach him except the men who taught him to speak and gave him language. And yet...they did not really teach him, they just talked and he followed. Now, the Kuan Yin tells him that he has great teachers.

Every night before he goes to bed and to sleep, he goes back into his beautiful, beautiful temple and he sits there in his quietness with his God, himself and the Kuan Yin. He hears singing like he has never heard before. Naibhu has become very clear...very, very clear in his role as a priest. He gets stronger every day, stronger in a quieter sense. His presence means more than what he says. With growing clarity, he knows there are still things that he does not understand. The Kuan Yin tells him about teachers. She tells him about great souls who will help him if he listens. He really does not understand.

He knows only people and Kuan Yin and God. This is all he knows. He is a little apprehensive about the teachers. Naibhu only knows to do it himself or to get someone else to do it. Yet he is beginning to see that with some things that happen he cannot say that he did it, or anybody did it. So, he sort of passes these off as divine, God-directed things.

Coming to him one night is a very ancient man, someone he has never seen before in his life. He is a very "ancient one" with a long beard who appears grand. He has great strength. He comes in every night. Naibhu sees him. He is a big man like his father. At first he thinks he is dreaming and yet this image is very real...like a father. Naibhu tells him he does not remember much of his father. The "ancient one" appears to him like the Kuan Yin, except he has lived with the Kuan Yin; he knows her. She is real to Naibhu while he is not sure about the "ancient one." Despite his doubt, each night he looks for him and if he does not come, Naibhu is very sad. It is as though he has filled the gap between the two Kuan Yins with a male image. He does not look like the Buddha. He is an "ancient one"...scholarly, draped in white, carrying a staff that he leans on gently but not totally. He always smiles a deep knowing smile at Naibhu. Naibhu asks the Kuan Yin if this is what she meant by his teachers and she says, "Yes, you are beginning to see." He says, "But who am I seeing?" and she says, "Each person must discover who he sees and talks with to learn. Teachers are not assigned or predetermined. They are chosen by the person because of his needs and the level of teaching that he is prepared for. Teachers change as wisdom grows. People can only learn from teachers who communicate on their vibrational level."

Naibhu's days become longer. Although his work becomes lighter, his days become longer. The children grow and illumine his life. One man with such a big family! The people of the community prosper. The people come from farther and farther away to see him. Occasionally he gives a lesson. Mostly he shares his insights and is radiant. He looks forward more and more to his evenings with the Kuan Yin and the "ancient one."

At night he spends long, long hours sitting in his temple in the presence of his teachers. It seems that the essence of this "ancient one" comes to him regularly. He is always there. Naibhu knows that he has some special messages for him and so he waits. He is patient and yet he does not receive a message. This one night he senses something. It is different than he has ever sensed before and he is not sure why. Before this marvelous ancient spirit became known to him, he had sensed him on the mountain. When he retreated from the camp outside the big city what he learned carried him on his journey. He had absorbed information that became his and he forgot the experiences which brought the information.

Now he finds himself reaching up... reaching up... looking... looking for something. It is like something reaching to him also. He does not know what this "ancient one" is to teach him but he senses a mutual attraction. He no longer wishes a solitary path and he has a companion who seems to want to be with him also. This man who comes to Naibhu feels him at the same time Naibhu is reaching out for something. Now there is another path...it is as though Naibhu has found something new—something very fresh and something very fragile. He senses that the wise one, or the "ancient one" reaches down to him, taking his hand at the same time as he reaches up, to show him something very new, so very, very new.

Naibhu knows he can do as he wishes. He remembers on the mountain that time when he was so confused, so unhappy. He seemed to break through to the place where there are many people. He went to a big temple that time as though something was driving him to it. But his experiences now are different. Naibhu has command and he can come and go wherever he wishes and this "ancient one" will show him how and where. He likes this because he has the choice and he is a leader. The old one shows him the further reaches of the path.

Chapter Thirty-Three

Naibhu is on the steps of his temple in his green robe. He surveys the lovely little gardens of rocks and flowers and small trees the children have planted around the temple. They are ecstatic as they watch their garden grow and soften the temple into the earth. Naibhu teaches them the love of beauty and how to bring beauty into their lives. For the children the planting of flowers is a peaceful and harmonious beginning.

Many people continue coming to the temple now, coming from great distances. Administering to people according to their needs constitutes most of Naibhu's work. He does work with the children early in the morning to see that things move ahead, and he tones with them in the late afternoon, but most of the days are now spent with the people from outside the village.

On this particular day, six young priests come. They

have on yellow saffron robes. Naibhu sees that they are disturbed men, small, wiry and angry. They come to the steps, and they demand a hearing. Naibhu is busy with his people. He is not interested in demands. He ignores them and continues with his work of listening and teaching. They chide him and make fun of his green robe. Where did he come from? Nobody ever saw a priest in a green robe. They create a ruckus. This upsets Naibhu and his people who have come a long way for help. Finally, he asks his people to wait for him to quiet the noise. He goes down the steps and tells the men that they are upsetting his very important work, that if they would move away, he would see them in time when he has finished with his people. The priests are very annoyed. They demand attention now! Naibhu becomes angry, and he commands them to cross the street and wait for him. He will be finished and he will talk with them. They are rude. They leave abruptly hurrying southward, the direction from which they came.

Naibhu is troubled because he knows this is not the end of them. He does not know what to do; he is apprehensive. These priests were different from all Buddhic priests he has seen. They are not peaceful, fulfilled men who are compassionate and wise. These are hostile, demanding men who seemed to indicate Naibhu had taken something from them.

The priests return the next day, only this time there are many more of them. They said that they have come from the Buddhist temple where they were trained as monks in the big city to the south where Naibhu had tended camels. They want to know by what authority he is a priest. They have come to take over his temple which they say belongs to their large temple; it was built years ago by their priests. They dismiss him as they start to angrily enter his temple. Naibhu bars the door. He tells them that no one goes into that temple except to praise God. He will not have his sanctuary contaminated by the rage and the hostility of these men. They tell him this temple is their temple and is always available to priests.

He says angrily, "Not this temple!" They do not get in. To retaliate they demand his attention immediately. He responds that he is not finished with his people, that whatever they want can wait until he can see them because his mission is to these people and not to them. He does not know who has sent them, but they also can wait. They again demand, "By what rights are you a Priest?" He answers, "By the rights of God, I have no other rights."

The people come all day and Naibhu never finishes. They come more than ever before. The temple is full of happy people, who are free to enter the temple to praise God. They have found something empowering on the steps of the Temple with Naibhu which they take inside with sounds of chanting and toning. They do not need him. They are making their own ceremony. The group of waiting priests become more and more infuriated. They chide him saying that this should not take place in a temple. Naibhu tells them to go away and not to bother him; he is busy.

Every night when the children come, Naibhu is troubled. They are their same happy selves; they come to tone at the end of the day and give thanks to God. Here are these little beings that are growing, thriving and happy, and yet his heart is heavy. Naibhu asks for help. He asks for help for himself because he is very angry, and he does not wish to be angry. He wants to continue this experience and live in peace with his people. It is difficult when these men are out there chiding—attacking. He has ordered them off the temple steps. He tells them as long as they are as they are, they cannot ascend into the temple, that they are trouble makers, that they are not there for any good.

Naibhu always plans to go and be with them, but the people come...and people come...and the people come. They seem to come from everywhere. Naibhu is working until very late. When the people are gone, the priests have gone also. The people seem to come in spite of the priests. One day the priests form a chain. There are more and more of them. They block the people as he watches. A mighty rage wells up in him, for he knows some of these people are in deep need. Naibhu moves down the steps with a rage, wanting to kill them all. He waits. He waits. The people will not cross the priests' barrier. Naibhu experiences a violence he has not felt since he killed and escaped from the insane prison. He goes to the barrier chain, seeing the priests as inferior, slimy things. He hates their horrible yellow robes! He takes two men by the shoulders, and with one thrust he tears their arms apart. He pushes them away and motions to the people, "You may come in." The people are afraid. The priests become violent. They start toward the temple, and he bars the door. He says, "You will not enter this threshold!" Naibhu is deeply anguished. He sends word to the people to tell the children not to come to the temple. The priests threaten him; they spit at him, but he stays in front of them at the door with his arms out stretched. They do not attempt to enter, and he does not attack although he wants to.

He enters the temple when they finally go away. He is very confused and he is violently angry. He talks to God who tells him he is right in refusing to let these priests into the temple. Naibhu says, "But I do not know what to do, there are more each day and they are getting more and more angry and full of rage!" God says that Naibhu can handle it. If he uses his spiritual power, he can help them. He must find out why they are so compelled and help them to better answers. But the solution must come Naibhu's way and not theirs. They are too driven to be thoughtful. This assurance gives Naibhu some peace for a little while. He is totally surrounded by light, and he knows that this power is the power of God and nothing can penetrate it.

He hurries out to oversee his little ones before they go to sleep because he knows how worried they will be because he has told them not to come for their daily prayers. Their fears are soon calmed as they share the excitement of their day and the beauty of their lives. Then he goes home.

He goes back to the temple with apprehension to talk with the Kuan Yin, to thank her and to be in touch with her beautiful vibrations. He tells God that he is trying as best he can, and he says that he has much to learn; that he is a man and that these feelings come surging up in him and he cannot seem to stop them. He will try to do right by them. He asks God to teach him before he goes astray; he tells God that he will learn.

He goes to bed, but he does not sleep well. He is very restless, very restless. He knows that there is something pending. He is up many times—checking—checking. He thinks he has to go talk with the priests. He just has to talk with them. He must tell them—he has to tell them. He knows that the next day he will see them...he will absolutely see them. When the people come, he will tell them that he has to talk with the priests, and he will correct them firmly.

He goes very early to get flowers for the Kuan Yin. He prepares for what is to be a beautiful day. He will talk to the priests about what he knows, what he sees, and how he was sent to this temple and how the children came. He will tell them the whole story. They will understand. Naibhu is full of light. He will tell them with love. They will understand and when they understand, he will invite them into the temple. Then they will chant and tone together.

He is out waiting, and waiting, and waiting for the priests. The priests do not come. He sees a few people, but he is looking for the priests. They do not come. He thinks something has happened. They will come tomorrow he is sure. His people do not come today either. He sits there on the steps, waiting. He waits and he waits and no one comes. Some children come and say that the priests are way down the road, busy stopping people. The people cannot even come near the temple, and they are becoming upset. Naibhu is unsure. He thinks that he will go to them. He will leave his temple, and he will go to them.

He goes and as he approaches them, they move away

from him. They scatter! They go down into the fields of the countryside. They scurry away like frightened mice, so he cannot talk with them. While he is gone, they move around the back side and set his temple on fire. He rushes back; people come and fight the fire with water they raise from the well. The fire is soon out, but his robes are burned. The walls and turret remain but are scarred by the smoke. Immediately he notices that the beautiful Kuan Yin's are gone. His precious symbols who beckoned to him when he first saw the crumbling temple, who were comfort to him and his people in the repair and dedication of this house of worship. They were not there. The sure, real structures that were always there when the "mystical lady" appeared to him in his consciousness to teach him—they were stolen. Instead, he experiences two open holes in the altar where the Kuan Yins had stood. He is devastated.

Quietly, he sends for his remaining people and his children. They all needed to be together and physically busy so that they would ruminate less. They clean away all the debris. He talks to each helper on the steps, saying that all humans are capable of this. Each one of them is as he is, a human being with powerful feelings, that emotions are one of the huge burdens that "man" has to bear, but "man" has not understood this burden. Humans do not have to lose their way, but those priests have lost theirs. They are to be forgiven because they do not know. He tells them that he will talk with the priests and they will change because he has a very powerful message that has come from God. It has to do with understanding humanness, understanding their human weakness and knowing that God gave them that power to maintain their lives and to manifest the God in themselves, to do great things. But sometimes they get lost. He remembers when he was lost and he had killed. The people are touched because they feel their human weakness simultaneously with their divine greatness, and they have not learned to be both at one time. He invites them into the temple to praise God for the strength God had given them.

It is a glorious, glorious feeling and a profound time for these loyal people and their dedicated priest. The temple is blackened but the spirits soar. This is even more important than the temple...when the soul takes wings. Naibhu knows that he carries a very important message to these people. His rage at injustice had infuriated the priests, and he knows that he has not done well with them. Naibhu has been given another lesson—a very important lesson—this deep emotional strength, the strength from rightness and guidance can also get in his way of effective leadership. It could get in the way of God's work, too. He knows rightness and he knows wrongness, and he also senses that he is a man who should have taught the priests, not infuriated them.

Naibhu was threatened when they attacked him. He felt his determined strength weakening. He thought that they somehow have something that Naibhu does not have. Naibhu is not accepted. They are official. Naibhu is nothing except a simple man. Way down deep, however, he has something these priests do not have, and this too infuriates them. There is a part of him that knows that he is sent there to teach the priests. Naibhu spends long hours talking to God about his problem. He talks to God, saying that it is his problem; it is not the problem of the priests. It is not the problem of the people. It is Naibhu's problem. He tells God, "But, I have no training. I have no background. I barely know my name. My name the "awaited one" was given by the people; they have named me and you ask me to teach the priests?" And God always answers, "Yes!"

Despite the profound affirmation from the highest source, Naibhu suddenly recognizes the reality of the charges; he is unprepared according to the official temple priests whom he has accepted as "God's official leaders." He has taken over a temple which belonged to others. In a sense, he stole it. He believed it belonged to the people, but now he learns it belongs to some rigid branch of Buddhism. Despite these facts, he repaired it when it was unusable, dedicated it with his own thoughts and provided the experiences for the people and a community to prosper and grow, yet he and the people were trespassing on a temple of Buddhism. Naibhu gave up. To have done differently would have required that Naibhu truly be the strength of God, manifested. That is an overwhelming burden to this humble human. Weakness and depression resulted from this unwise thinking.

Chapter Thirty-Four

The saffron priests are gone. No one has seen them for days. The stillness in the air is like the lull before the second part of a great hurricane. There seems to be something pending that Naibhu is very aware of, and yet there appears to be no realistic danger. There are no priests to cajole him or threaten him. All is very quiet.

The people have returned to the temple where he meets them each day on the steps. They come regularly to pray and give thanks for their happiness and the plenty of their land. They have more skills to solve their problems themselves, so Naibhu's early morning teaching on the steps has dwindled. They love their temple and maintain it. The sides are always banked with flowers. The fire soot has been removed. They still fill the vases between where the Kuan Yins were.

Naibhu seems more mellow than he has been as

though he has aged rather rapidly in some way. He greets the people with a warmth and mellowness that Naibhu has rarely shown consistently. There is a softness in his way, a smoothness in his movement, and yet he works with people more effectively than he has ever worked with them. The people bring warmth and understanding. He loves them and they are healed. They find a freshness in life and excitement in looking ahead. The temple literally vibrates with love. He wonders if his earthly time is short. The fullness that has come to him and to the people as the result of this temple and its opportunities are now relished by both without knowing what will happen in the future.

It is autumn of the year. The mellowness of the land is a ripeness that is softer than the freshness of the spring; it is also richer. He sees the remaining children late in the day. Many have grown up and returned to their families' villages. Others have become farmers elsewhere. A few of the youngest ones remained. They are housed in the better homes doing domestic work. Naibhu has no children who need him.

Naibhu goes not too far from the temple in these days. He recalls when it was burned. Although the temple structure is sill intact there remains some damage. So he goes as far as the farm place where the children used to live. He does not teach them as much any more. But he watches them, and he sees the crowning beauty of God's great masterpiece, the children, and he remembers the time on the temple steps and the deep sadness in their faces, the destruction of their bodies and their lack of hope. Now he sees all that absolutely reversed in their joy of exuberant life. Naibhu releases these children to their own development. He has taught them well. They work. They seem to be under their own power now and not his. He is happy about that. They still come each evening to the temple to give prayers of thanks and to tone. Little is needed from Naibhu. Each child can communicate with God and receive guidance without him. He is always there to share their radiance and marvel at the divine plan operating.

Still, there is prevailing sadness in Naibhu. In most of his life there has been the excitement of something new, a new struggle, that stimulated his energy. Now that seems to have come to a close. He spends longer hours in the temple alone. He is much closer to God than he has ever been. And each day seems to renew and strengthen that relationship. There is not much need. Naibhu asks for less and receives more. At times he experiences a deep spilt—one side is richness and contentment, the other is deep anxiety. He wonders if life will be terminated abruptly, possibly at the hands of the priests. He desperately wants an opportunity to talk with them and to teach them. He recalls his mistakes when he asked them to wait until he finished with his people. In truth they are also his people.

He has made a big mistake. Although the priests came with hostility, he sensed that they needed him as much as the other people. The difference is that the other people know they need him, but these priests do not know they need him; he does not seem to bridge the gap, knowing that while they came with one intent, there is another one which he should have acknowledged. He sees this now deeply and he is troubled by it. He needs them as much as they need him. He hopes he will have the opportunity to talk with the priests again. Yet another part of him believes that the opportunity may be gone.

He goes about his work even more deeply than before. He knows more than he has ever known. He has a gentleness within him. He speaks less and directs less, but Naibhu is being more than he had been. He does not have to speak as much. He teaches in other ways. When he sits with people, he leads them into spiritual experiences by his presence. He lets all of them know that it is their experience and not his and that it is available to them at all times. This is the level of his teaching.

Naibhu no longer sleeps in his little back room because it was burned and not repaired. Also, he does not wish to be there any more. He sleeps quietly sitting in the temple. The Kuan Yin is very close to him most of the time. He wears his green and purple robes. His brown one was tattered and burned in the fire. He does not miss it nor need it, for Naibhu is not doing physical work any more. As he sits in the temple, he hears etheric music which seems to play all of the time. He sees spiritual beings who surround him. He believes a new kind of experience is coming.

He enters another spiritual level...one that has deep stillness to it and great pensiveness. He is aware at times of the human anxiety that seems to rise in him with a faint knowing that he may be going to die violently at the hands of the priests. At other times, he has a passive knowing that dying is just another level of his ultimate life. There are other times in which his pervading struggle for his life becomes so charged that Naibhu wants to fight. Occasionally he is torn by these two ways of being that go back and forth. He experiences these completely but is not overwhelmed! He thinks and recalls his life struggles which were followed by a deep quietness and a sweet understanding. Naibhu is preparing for his ultimate growth and these are his struggles.

The children notice changes in Naibhu. His great enthusiastic happiness that he has shared with them seems less. He is more pensive and quiet. He talks less. They come around him to give him assurance that they love him. They sit and put their small hands on his knees. They are the great healers! When they come into the temple, they too feel more and talk less to Naibhu. They are very subtle, very expressive and very tender.

Naibhu is sad to see that the children are affected by his deep pensive moods at these times. Yet he realizes that this is a part of their learning also; life is not always full of joy. There are times when humans learn the most when they experience themselves deeply, their own feelings about life. Naibhu is honest and he allows his little ones to see him as he is. They watch him intently.

Naibhu wonders. He wonders because he is coming

closer and closer to God in a deeper and all pervasive way. It seems that God comes within him. He has total peace at times but it does not hold constantly because he finds the other side of himself which he knows well, that cries out for recognition. That part of him exclaims, "Do not forget me, too. I am a human and I have needs." Naibhu struggles with these voices. He prays and he experiences. He has no answer, and yet he does not deny this most profound knowledge of human life—to encompass and be both human and divine.

Chapter Thirty-Five

On the surface Naibhu's life has never been so complete and free from cares or so rewarded. All changes that he has started in the community now progress without him, yet he is always available to his people. The hostile priests have not returned. He spends long hours in the temple alone, blending with God. Often his life experiences flash into his mind as clearly as when he lived them. Then he needed understanding...now he has profound insight into his life's patterns and unfoldment. Recall is not orderly—it comes randomly, one thing leading to another but not as it happened. Threads seem to activate his memory. He remembers the time he went away to the mountain near the big city where he had found God, the mountain where he had discovered with Juda how to find joy and freedom and God's guiding hand before the drowning, and when he went into the mountains before he came to the power of God to heal and lead the temple beggar children, and even back further, to his life as a small child who hid in the mountains, who learned the ways of the wilderness and the living things which dwelled there and nourished him.

Naibhu goes back to the times he has wandered; he was always a wanderer, a seeker. He remembers the difference between running and wandering. The earliest times he wandered and looked in search of food; next he wandered to discover the world and them to find his mission; now he has the urge to wander again. But this time he knows that wandering is the way his mind can be cleared from all responsibility, so he can transcend his earthly being and contact and love the soul that gives him life.

He stops his reminiscence long enough to go to his children to tell them that he is going away for a while. They do not need him in the same way now, and he will be back. Then he goes to the nearest farmhouse to borrow a goat companion. For so much of his life goats accompanied him. He chooses a young goat...they are better company and always stay close by. He takes nothing else with him but his simple white clothes like those all men wear. The robes he leaves in the temple; he will wander as the simple man that he is, without acknowledgment of the man he has become.

He comes to rocks where he sits down with the little goat at his feet. He recalls that much of his life has been spent climbing upward over rocks. Just to be on top of even a small pile of rocks makes him feel grand and high. But as he sits there, Naibhu experiences considerable difficulty. For a while all he notices is fear and anger. Then with an explosion of energy, he relives that terrible episode in the tiny village where he had run after escaping the prison. This is the first time he had become a leader of people who seek his help with animals and growing things. There is goodness in this memory that he wishes to prolong but he cannot. He remembers these same loving people taking him before a hostile tribunal that condemned him. Then more clearly than he has ever recalled, he is again racked up on the goat stretcher. He even remembers that his body does not hurt very much, only his mind suffers as he watches from a higher place the confusion of these people. He watches as they condemn him after he has confessed his story of killing.

Naibhu did not struggle against hanging because he felt so overwhelmingly guilty. His hanging was his punishment. He wanted to suffer to remove his guilt. He needed punishment for his impulsive act of killing to save his life. This time he will not repeat his error; he will die quietly. At that instant his intense "will," a "will" to live and to be free, comes over him again. It passes quickly. Then he remembers that as he fell to the ground, he had the sudden thought, "I did not do that. I did not experience the "will" to live and tear myself loose!" He remembers crawling toward safety where they would not find him underneath the vines. Now he again feels the intense soreness of his regained awareness of a body that barely moved. The ability and strength he developed in boyhood seemed replaced with a strange body that does not work. It looked the same despite his bruises and scratches. He remembers running, running and running again.

It seems that wherever he had gone until now there was this intense running. Again his life has been spared and he has regained his will to live. Then he does not ask the question, "Why has he been spared?" Now he knows that the deepest part of his soul needed to live in this body to do its final work.

Naibhu thinks how strange that he can remember now, but he cannot prolong the memory of the agony. Now these memories serve him differently, not as hurdles to overcome but as markers and reminders of the torturous path his soul has chosen. He knows these experiences are chosen in the sense that he needs powerful motivations to keep him on track.

Then his recall centered around restlessness; restlessness drove him to wander and to learn and know about people, cities, money, food and clothing. He thinks that he was restless to gain information about all of those things. And now he knows that these are needs and wants of his flesh and not his soul. His basic restlessness arises from the destiny his soul has chosen for its material life. Then, because he knew not his destiny, his life's pattern seemed devious. Somehow he knows that destiny needs a life to be its vehicle...without life he cannot complete anything! He realizes suddenly now that his "will" gets caught up in living and loses sight of its primary mission to grow in divine spirit while still human. He has moved on and learned lessons, often unimportant ones. Now he is wandering again...not searching but taking time to integrate and understand himself in the highest realms.

The day is closing and the richness of the autumn amber ignites the countryside providing a mellowness for his soul's integration. Naibhu returns his primary awareness to the night, food for the goat and where he will sleep out of sight of those who people the roads at anytime. He leaves the road going west up a dry creek bed, away from the inhabited areas. It is pleasant land stretching on both sides, rolling but not steep, appearing to have been planted eons ago but now returning to its native state of grasses and small shrubs. His body quickens to the beauty of this golden amber light that radiates everywhere. He knows he will not go far...he will sleep in the soft grasses with nothing above him but the infinite twinkle of the heavens. Never has he experienced such contentment. The needs of his body-self blend with his soul-self, imperceptibly. He wants to stay awake to remember this state of perfection, as though it may slip from him before he has totally absorbed its full essence. He lies with his large frame outstretched, crushing the grass to a soft stable bed. The little goat likes it too and jumps and scampers around him...stopping only to nibble.

Naibhu slips unknowingly back and forth in levels of his consciousness. Each stage completely serves his needs of the moment. The night is perfect for him. As sunrise comes, lighting the country with a silver streak, he plays with his companion who had snuggled close and quietly beside him as he slept. The goat energetically eats from everything. Naibhu is fasting. He sits quietly before he stands...each level giving him new sights and smells that he savors. Whatever is to be his day is not governed by time. Slowly he picks his way farther up the creek bed, marveling at the rock formations and seeing the land as it had been many centuries before and how it will be many centuries later. He is in that state to contemplate the material world without barriers of time before, after and beyond. Walking seems to unfocus and refocus nature in this mind's experience.

He finds moist places where simple digging brings enough water to quench their thirsts. Later in the day he comes to a tumbled pile of rocks where the creek bed takes a sudden turn. Here he can see off in the distance to clumps of trees, rippling land and a few perfectly related hills. His vision stretches out in all directions. The goat scrambles to the top. He is content to climb part way so as not to displace nature's arrangement with his heavy weight. He settles comfortably in a formation shaped to his half reclining body where he can stare upwards and off across the horizon without moving. He reverts immediately to the reminiscence of the preceding day.

He sees himself again in the big city where he thinks he will remain and satisfy his needs. He recalls his restlessness to move on and searches elsewhere. He remembers the little baby goat Juda who chose him and taught him to love again. He sees again how very dejected he had been. Here when he has a free life, food, work and sufficient money, he has nothing that he seeks. He remembers how God came and talked to him up in those rocks and how his life was changed as if by miracle. He, Naibhu, had changed from that moment on. He knows God...no one ever has to tell him or remind him again...such reality has penetrated his being. He is no longer here to preserve his life, to learn, to speak and feed himself, but forever to grow in God's light toward his human greatness.

He now knows that his destiny extends beyond the being of Naibhu with personal needs. He remembers leaving the encampment and following a direction blindly; blindly yet clearly, he was led northward into a land where he had never been. He remembers how perfectly and gently he had been guided to everything. He knows he has participated with God at every turn and that he is not blindly directed. He recalls how good people have been to him; how they want to be with him. He sees himself doing his first teaching on the steps of the temple and realized he had found his way.

He smiles as he sees Juda and the little girl who is nearly grown now. Both are very happy together. Yes, his images are more than simple recall now; he can see all he wishes to see, beyond the facts to their meanings. And then the dead little boy; he remembers the surge of power that came through him when he went down among the grieving people to recover Juda. He experiences the little girl who crawled up to grasp his leg—how he picked her up to quiet her sobbing. Again he sees himself holding his hands over the boy's head to bless him as he had always done with dead goats. This time he sees the boy returning to life and remembers with great joy. Then he had run away from this chance to comprehend the majesty and mystery of life. He now sees the magnificence of such an experience and thanks God for allowing him to participate. He wishes he had more chances to serve. He sees that boy, a man now, with a young family of his own.

Finally, he recalls first finding the little temple all in disrepair and abandoned and how he knew he had found his home. He sees again the people rebuilding their temple while he watches and motivates them.

With pleasure he recalls his stumbling yet always successful efforts to serve and learn to be a priest-teacher. His largest problem then was trusting his knowing. He briefly experiences the "fever" that nearly took his life and the powerful insights about the human "will."

He thinks about the great surge in his priesthood coming from his circle trip. After he had repaired the temple and was ready to start his work, he recognized that he did not know how to be a priest. It was then that he took the circle trip to clear his mind. He remembers going from place to place never seeking but always finding human problems that needed his help. He remembers the village where no one talked to another outside of the immediate family and how his work with little children brought love instead of hate. He remembered the great surge of joy that came to him on the mountain when love of mankind overwhelmed him.

He remembers vividly coming to the big old temple with the maimed children and his wrath when he entered such ugliness, the people walking by and evading recognition of the children beggars. He saw again a tiny baby girl in a basket. She had a mangled arm and was tended by a slightly older sister. He carried the basket and infant all the way back to his temple; she was too small to walk. This same girl now brings him single flowers and a loving kiss each day. Suddenly he recalls the group healing of these children...his amazement. And how he sat all night with his energy and cloak making a protective umbrella of shelter. He remembers the power that came through him that day never really left him. Glimmers of the small boy traveling on the caravan with his mother and his successful attempt to run away interspersed with his other thoughts but never lingered long.

These were mere physical and emotional hardships that strengthened his body and "will" for the continued learning he would seek in the future. These no longer fit into the soul's clarification.

He remembers when he returned to the temple with his children. He knew how to perform his priestly duties and to accept his responsibilities to serve his people. He had talked with his people as he taught them to value the temple and their own judgment. This was when people stopped bowing down to anything. They do not even bow down to the Kuan Yin; instead they love her and talk with her.

Naibhu remembers with great joy the things that seemed to just happen in his life. He now has insight about them. Tears of recognition spread over his face and peace comes in abundance. It is as though the meaning of his life has totally opened to him. The intense directions that his life has taken has been overwhelming. His motivations have been so powerful, focusing every single experience. He has compulsively tackled what he has had to do. Nothing deterred him as he went about his work. However, each time he was not totally successful.

Now he knows that all effort which seemed sidetracked into other paths and ways of expression was necessary for his growth. This was his life's way of pursuing his destiny. Without this evolving plan, Naibhu could have had even greater difficulty.

Naibhu came into this lifehood with an almost impossible job. To make change in human thought as in his own about the true meaning of life and human divinity. He brought an intense "will," an immense energy, a profound dedication to seek the God within him. If his life had been a pleasant and easy one, he would surely have abdicated such a lofty goal. Naibhu now recognizes he has accomplished much against what seemed impossible barriers. He has prevailed and he was winning the ultimate prize of self-knowing and the reason for human existence. He wonders if his work is complete.

Again the day closes as he retraces his steps to the grassy pad his body had shaped the night before. His awareness is no longer locked in time as these days fuse past, present and future. His night is even more profound than before when space and time blended into cosmic wholeness, "everything is everything and all is perfect."

As daybreak comes Naibhu is refreshed and ready to return to his temple, his people and his priestly duties. He walks briskly back to the road greeting every traveler with his cheery message and radiance. The goat scampers to his home with a final glance at the big man who took him for an outing. Naibhu checks in with the children and hurries to his morning work with his people.

Chapter Thirty-Six

As Naibhu returns to his temple, he realizes that he has put together some things that have lain dormant in his mind for all these years. He puts on his green robe and waits on the temple steps ready for his people. Naibhu glows like he has never glowed before. Then some things happen that have never happened to him before. Naibhu is not afraid to lay on hands. He moves amongst his people more aggressively than he has ever done before and yet with more peace. He knows that the strength of human beings is because they carry God within them. All the weakness his human feeling has brought to him seems turned around. It is the weakness in life that humans can change.

At night he sits in his temple—not because he is afraid but because he does not wish to sleep. He wishes to experience and savor the beauty that has come into his life and he does not wish to sleep it away. So he mostly stays in a euphoric state. Sleep seems unimportant. The great spiritual ones visit Naibhu, making the temple always full. He is never, never alone. A celebration is surely happening. The days pass slowly; restlessness returns to Naibhu. He sees his children each morning; he shares excitement with their learning and growing, and yet his heart is heavy. He cannot concentrate. The children particularly notice his restlessness and come to him with lovingness. They too sense some great change occurring in him.

Each day he sees his people on the steps where he teaches, listens and shares his growing wisdom. But he seems more remote from their problems. He eats sparingly, for his mind is not of these things; his thoughts drift to ultimate things. The Kuan Yin is always with him. In the evening time after he has eaten simple grain and seeds, he goes to the temple to be with companions. The "ancient one" comes to comfort him and the Kuan Yin is ever present.

Naibhu is torn with strange intense feelings. When a divine vibration seems to fill him, earthly cares disappear. But at times fear and anxiety seem to come from nowhere, taking over, reminding him of his human mortality. He spends every night in the temple, never returning to his bed of straw. Here he will prolong his closeness with God. He thinks, how strange that he feels more comfortable when anxiety wracks him. Time is endless.

One night as he moves into that blissful spiritual state, he becomes aware of noises outside the temple...soft muffled sounds of beings moving in from all directions. He awaits even afraid to open his eyes, to test the reality of what he already knows. As the noise grows closer...inside the temple...he is compelled to see. The room fills with men pouring through the doors and windows until his space gets smaller and smaller and he is surrounded.

He recognizes the priests who have harassed him but

have silently left some time ago. This time there are others, common people in white clothes but all with the same intense determined hostile expression. They circle him and move him to the center, jostling, threatening and condemning. Naibhu is not frightened; he is comforted and sustained by God. His earlier anger at these people is gone; he feels he is their teacher, and although he believes that his life may be taken, he is unafraid. He is even happy to have the chance to tell them about himself, an opportunity he thinks he had lost by his anger. Now he has it again.

As he sits in the center of the temple, he is sure and clear. He feels the hostility and rage of the men but it does not affect him. At first everyone speaks at the same time, but quietly; there is no shouting. Attack after attack bounces off him. He has no tears and no emotion except love for these misdirected men.

A crippled priest leads a "mock trail" attacking him for his practice, asking where he got his training, and accusing him of believing in a supreme being, a single God and leading his people to accept that man is God. Naibhu does not understand their motives and only one attack stuck—he is not an ordained Buddhic Priest yet he poses as one.

Naibhu chooses to answer their attacks only briefly. What is more important is to share with them his incredible journey from childhood. They listen. His voice is firm and commanding; his words are simple and direct and around him arises such a glow that the temple lights in all corners. When he first speaks, he admits that he has no training except from a divine source. He says he was called by God to the priesthood. He says he has never been schooled. He has no formal training as a priest. He has never read the great writings...in fact, he does not know how to read. He admits to knowing nothing about training temples where priests learn or about the book of Buddha. He tells them he has been in very few temples until this, his own.

He reiterates that he entered the world at this time to

bring spiritual enlightenment, and this goal has been strengthened by his Buddhist priest father. He relates to them what a struggle his life has been just to exist in the mountains alone with goats...without a high purpose. He tells of his stealing from the caravans and his escape to the village with the temple where he touched the Buddha's foot and felt such great, great power. Quickly he relates the story of the insane prison where he learned to speak. Now his voice changes to a sweet spiritual tenor as he tells them when God came to him in the mountains when his "will" to live was waning and of how God's message sent him on his journey north, blindly yet with utmost clear directions. And when he came to this shell of a temple, he knew the course of his life was a priest-teacher. All this he shares with loving warmth.

The men's postures somewhat soften; the lines in their faces calm. Whether they hear his story or feel his being...the attacks abate. The quietness makes his words echo and penetrate.

He confesses that he has not always been sure of what he should say or do as a priest. What he does say comes to him from other levels and from the "great", the "ancient one," and from the Kuan Yin, whom he has known as the "beautiful lady" since he was a small boy. Most of all his information comes directly from God. All the men listen...some of the older priests are touched. He is amazed because he first told them, "I cannot answer your questions. I can only tell you my story. I do not know the answers to your questions. Only recently have I been aware of why I am here and exactly what happened in my life."

He talks to them about the long time of doubt that he should lead these people. How he has gone up into the mountains and again contacted God. He is sent back down to the temple with an even bigger understanding of faith and that somehow he is truly a priest in the full sense.

Suddenly as Naibhu's story comes to the present time, he begins to feel and show insecurity. As he hesitatingly talks about his healings, his voice becomes unsteady—he is not sure. He even confesses that he does not understand or believe what occurred, but he does witness it. At times he is totally sure and at others he is equally unsure. He doubts this healing power, and he fails to recognize that God serves through him.

He tells them that he has been very close to God, and he feels God in him. He does not have to pray to God, and he does not have to talk to God; he just is with God. These very true and positive statements bring forth their opposites. All his unanswered questions about his relationship to God come forth. He knows his divine nature at times, recognizing and owning the power. Then he understands that mankind could only know God operating through them not outside them. For Naibhu such divine states are not permanent but off and on. There are still hidden pockets of doubt about God's influence and his relation to humans, particularly to him.

As he comes to the stage of his doubts, Naibhu loses his power. He falters. The angry priests who were starting to change hearing Naibhu's tenderness and sincerity are now moved toward their hostile and revengeful states. Naibhu becomes weaker...the radiance diminishes from his being. Although more glowing, it is no larger than his coercers. They attack him violently, saying that no human is God. They become more and more agitated, condemning him for being false and desecrating a temple. He must pay for his horrendous deeds with his life. What had started as true teaching for these priests in the beginning has been weakened. Naibhu knows that he does not have the strength that he hoped for. He had started out to teach and change these hostile priests, but instead he has now shared his weaknesses. A flash of his childhood appears when he was charged to serve people, to lead them into spiritual insights. Now, strangely he feels he has not led them very far.

The priests find the moment when they move in with

attack...verbally and physically. They grab him! They call him a fake and a destructive man. The power comes back to Naibhu, but it is all physical power. He flails and he knocks people all over the room. They swarm over him like insects. They secure him by sheer numbers and they bind him. His hands behind his back, his legs together; they bind him! They wrap him up like a mummy. So his entire body is bound. He can barely breathe. He is tied up in his beautiful temple. Someone gets a big stone and hits him in the head and knocks him out. He is lost in a stupor state. He cannot move. Then they lift him outside and dump him in a cart. Naibhu does not struggle now...somehow he feels less than worthy in God's eyes—he passively accepts his punishment. Many of the men leave...their work is done; some young priests and a few very ancient men mill around awaiting something.

Periodically Naibhu is not aware of his body. He remains in a half aware state slipping back and forth from divine states of selflessness, without ordinary sensations, to human states of seeing his body bound and pained. On first light of dawn before the villagers stir, a large bullock drawn cart comes near. He knows that he will be transported somewhere, but he has no energy or "will" to contest.

Instead of hoisting him into the cart they unstrap his legs, remove his sandals and tie him to the back of the cart to walk on the rough rock road bed. Native peoples walked on the road edges on paths worn smooth by bare feet and soft sandals. The road was deeply gutted from cart wheels, hoof marks and rocks dumped during the monsoon seasons. He was tied so close to the cart he could not see to choose best where to step.

They turned east through the little village where he first found people hating each other, where he first taught little children to love, where he realized that the children where his apostles. Many of these people later traveled to worship at his temple. When they approach a village, he is placed back in the cart and wrapped in a shroud, his face covered with a cloth. The broad daylight brought curious onlookers. The cortege stopped at each village to announce that Naibhu was very ill. They were taking him to the great temple on the main north-south road. This was the circle route that Naibhu had traveled where he was to learn how to be a priest after his temple restoration. The priests said that Naibhu would be healed there or if he died before reaching the temple there would be the place for his pyre. Temporarily the village people blocked the road way to pay homage to Naibhu, telling the priests how Naibhu had improved their lives.

At every village where the cortege stopped the young priests stood in stately form at the sides and back of the cart obscuring a clear view. The elderly priests riding the cart further blocked people from clearly seeing Naibhu. Because this cortege was so official, no one peered under the cloth that covered his face. And because of the size of the body in the cart, they knew it was Naibhu. Before the cortege reached a settlement, the grapevine messages told of his coming. People meet the cortege with weeping and wailing. Naibhu knows of their grief but he weakens. The pain and swelling in his feet, the lack of food and water and his depression drain his strength. The priests keep him riding in the cart more of the time now.

Chapter Thirty-Seven

Naibhu's altered state is just high enough to escape his mind and body torment; he has not reached the level of ascension. His soul seems to know he has to lead and teach again before melding with the vibrations of God. The old priests talked amongst themselves. Naibhu hears and realizes why he was taken from his temple and what were the strong emotional motivations of the young priests. It seemed that more young men were entering the Buddhic training schools than ever before. Upon their ordination, they yearned for a temple to teach their compelling beliefs. But there were no free temples. The older priests recalled building Naibhu's temple years ago and allowing it to deteriorate when there were no priests to sustain it. They also remembered that the large temple which was built by a cult of Hindus had partly accepted Buddhic faiths from their "pagan" beliefs of many deities, gods and serpents. They heard that someone had destroyed the inside at a time when there was no Buddhic priest to reactivate their beliefs. The older priests were along to insure that the young priests be crusaders to take over these temples without violence.

Naibhu realizes sadly that his temple belongs to the line of Buddhic priests whose predecessors built the temple. Now when there were many trained priests, they reclaimed his temple. Naibhu listens intently - energy surges back to him. He asks the old priests to tell him about Buddha and his teachings. They are happy to share. This is what he learns! Buddha was a nobleman, a Hindu who had grown up with the teaching of many gods, some divine and some disruptive. Hindus spent their lives trying to appease spiritual beliefs that tugged from all sides. Man was "will-less" as he sought to follow the gods' needs as their own. Buddha was not content with these beliefs and their effects upon followers. He was intolerant of the dependency encouraged by the gods who could bring forth stress and destruction. He left his wealthy holdings to quietly wander, meditate and seek the truth for man to live by. After many years he reached enlightenment. From a state of peaceful insight he brought forth noble truths, steps along the paths and meditative states. The basic tenets of Buddha were few: to live each day with truth, to seek wisdom and compassion for one's fellow men and all living things.

Naibhu learns from the priests that Buddhism with emphasis upon direct experience had little concern with ideas or concepts. Therefore it has no concept of God. Naibhu is confused. He had experienced God. Buddhic beliefs did not recognize an immortal soul which did not concern him. He had not pondered past lives. They believe that the highest reality was emptiness. Contrary to earlier Hindu beliefs, they believe nirvana is here and now. Believers did not need to escape the world. Naibhu senses that the old priests were trying to tell him that there is nothing left to master if one has control over his mind. He did not like that idea for he did not wish to give up his brilliant, rational way of handling things totally to the intuitive, imaginative, mystical way. For he believed that persons who escape from reality would always feel the terror of reality when answers do not exist.

Naibhu likes that Buddha gave no obedience to particular rituals or commandments from gods or a single being from above. He never used a ritual for he had discovered what worked with him and his people to be ever changing. He clung to believing in a deep sensation of self, although he lost the self concept with all its values of worth.

The priests explain that Buddha realized that most people's lives were full of frustrations and sufferings in attempts to solve unsolvable problems. If one forgot the past and lived for today not the future, the stress was lessened...for yesterday was only a memory, tomorrow but a vision. Look well to today; suffering came through clinging to ideas and people to solve problems. Naibhu realizes that he had inhaled everything, his and the troubles of the world. For this he needed to exhale a lot. Buddha described that one must not cling to a state of nirvana but be able to give up one's life to save it. Suddenly Naibhu has a profound insight and wonderment. He asks the old priests if the reason Buddha had not envisioned a one divine being, a single God was because he wanted to break the deep dependency the people had on many gods who controlled them and dominated their thoughts? If he just transferred cultural beliefs about many gods to a one God, the problems would remain. The old priests look at him quizzically; no one had ever talked about why Buddha brought forth what he did, only that it worked with the people at that time. Naibhu is so happy that his relationship with his God is an empowering one, not one of humbling dependency. As Naibhu heard the clear tenets of Buddha, he knew that Buddha had touched the divine vibrations which to him was a one God. Naibhu has another wonderment of why Buddha did not believe in reincarnation or an after life. Was it to counteract the

Hindu beliefs that if man suffered enough in this life, he would be rewarded in afterlife with a state of "nirvana?" By Buddha's emphasis upon life now — no past, no future, no afterlife — troubled concerns and practices of suffering would be mitigated and man's energy could now be used without consulting his memories or living in doubt. Again the old priests have no answers to Buddha's motivations. Naibhu is satisfied because by posing the questions clearly, he had found his answer.

The cart creaks on in human silence, no one speaks. Their deep sharing is over. Both Naibhu and the old Buddhic priests know they are talking about their common experiences, that somehow spirituality was built-in to humanness. Both had transcended the dogmas of religions. An abrupt change in the cortege's direction signals their destination. The procession turns south again toward the large old temple where he smashed the Buddha and healed the children. He wonders if this is where he could be sacrificed. His mind waits for whatever is next. Naibhu thinks he can never be hurt again...he has transcended the physical life even before his spirit departs. Time drags on without recognition.

Finally, as they ascend a small hill, he sees in the far distance the old temple with the ugly paintings of serpents. He senses that the cortege is awaited by the townspeople. Faintly, he remembers their wrath when he tried to return their healed children. Mostly he recalls his own rage.

As the afternoon comes they stop more often, this time to revive Naibhu to put water in his mouth and bathe his face. Obviously they want to keep him alive. Before they reach the large temple on the slow ascension up the hill, the priests relay a startling fact. They say that the people at this temple placed one Buddhic statue among the gods, serpents and banners inside their temple. They often injured their children to make them beggars on the temple steps, believing if the child suffered in this life, he would pay back his karma and could reach "nirvana" after death. Yes, they wanted money from their children's begging, but primary was their beliefs that their sufferings assured peace and plenty in afterlife. Naibhu suffers pangs of contrition. Now he knew how brash he had been to punish them and tear up their temple. He had not understood that they were in mortal transition between ancient tenets of Hinduism and the fresh thoughts of Buddha.

Naibhu excitedly shares his direct experiences with God. He glows and radiates as he does. He is now a teacher again sharing his beliefs with the old priests who listen as attentively as he had. He tells about the "beautiful lady," which he learned they called "Kuan Yin." He talks excitedly about the times he had been pulled to the Buddhic temple. He recalls his father a Buddhic priest whom he followed without thought while he performed his priestly duties.

As they near the temple, he hears shouts of welcome, as if the townspeople have awaited this time, knowing the priests would bring Naibhu. This then would be their time to take revenge upon him for his destruction of their temple and taking their children. Twelve or thirteen years have lapsed since that day. He believes that their wrath has not lessened with time, that they lust to personally kill him. This ghastly trip has prepared him to know their vengeance.

The cortege stops in front of the temple steps, the ones where he found his children, where they slept all night under his protective cover. Many people rush in toward him; the surge of energy revives him, so that he is able to rise to a partial sitting position with his tied knees protruding almost to his head, not his favorite Lotus position but at least more upright. A golden radiance encases everyone with a great beam resting on his dusty, bloody body. He has never felt the spirit of God so magnificently. The people hold sticks, clubs and rocks to pummel him. But first they want to verbally castigate him. He does not hear what they say, for he is preparing to speak to them. And he does with his firm, soft, resonant voice that commands their quiet listening.

He smiles and thanks them for coming to see him. He had hoped to return a long time ago to repair their temple and beg their pardon for his transgressions. He wants most of all to tell them about their beautiful children, so he does not wait for their response. Immediately and with animation, he tells them about each child and how strong he is and how large. Some have already left the group to have their own farms and families. He tells them how the remaining children, all teenagers, live and how much they mean to the community by their work and happiness. He knows that a few of his children have returned to this village to help their parents. He relates the glorious times they have all had in the temple at the close of the day when they toned and knew God's glory in their own lives. He praises them and says that the opportunity these people have given him to heal and raise their children has been the most important gift in his life. He thanks them deeply for sharing.

He continues aware that the angry expressions on the people's faces have begun to soften. Their threatening hands holding their weapons have relaxed to their sides. A strange, quizzical expression indicates that they are thinking. He tells them that he knows how difficult it is to change the cultural dictates that they have grown up with and what stress it had been to have more and more children to feed each year with no work for them to do. He understands why they had turned some children to begging. And he knew that handicapped children touched the heartstrings of givers more than normal children. These things he understands and so does God. He adds that such thoughts must have gone through the mind of each parent when he made that emotional decision to injure his child or children. Also he knows that some of these children might not have lived had they not begged and brought in money to the family. Further he adds that for as long as history had created these problems, people have made decisions of what to do. And because many throughout the ages have decided upon this way it is easier for each generation to come to the same conclusion. This ready-made solution had spared them the emotional anguish of thinking through these old errors in judgment and making a higher, but possibly unpopular choice.

The crowd's mood is dramatically changing. He hears the stones that they hold hit the ground as their hands relax. He has opened to their awareness the sensitive problem of all people, the torment of going along with ancient patterns because these exist, in spite of the inevitable emotional burdens these present. Change is the hardest. Their choice had been the easier way.

But he goes on to remind them that all humans know the divine law, the primary measure for judgment. He recognizes profound sadness has been theirs for denial of these laws.

He continues that the violence they have expressed to him when he tried to return their children was surely not because their children were now better, possibly cured. It must have been because to have accepted the cured child would have demanded that they change and refute their cultural ways. Few people have such strength.

He recognizes that their deep love brings guilt for their acts that return to haunt them. He confesses that if he had been a wiser priest at that time he could have helped them to a deeper understanding of these emotions with more appropriate behavior. Naibhu's teaching is over, and there are tears in all eyes, many sobbing openly. Now their faces register the anguish of misdirection with the recognition that they have given up their strength and fallen prey to mass beliefs. While it eased burdens temporarily, in another sense it brought long-time suffering which they did not understand.

The group mills around and away from him. Before they disband he feels one last surge of power. He tells them where their children are, and he suggests they might want to go see them for themselves to ask for their forgiveness and to again feel their love. He tells them that their little ones are so happy, he is sure they can help them with forgiveness. This way is the best way to truly lighten their burdens.

He asks them to please not leave until they have heard his confession. "Your children are the first group I ever helped God to heal; it was such a shock and surprise to me. I was so apprehensive with that seemingly inhuman power. The anger I expressed to you parents came to me from my fears of this totally divine power. It was my anger then that caused me to see ugliness in your temple and to smash your precious Buddha image."

He knows that these people forgive him as they slowly creep away. Some come near him, a few touch his soaked clothes, many weep. Several of his former children, young adults now, come forward from the crowd to embrace him and tell him how much they missed him. They tell him of their work to heal the community; how they have been given leadership roles and how the older people listen to their stories of their learning about God and love. Now Naibhu weeps with joy and humility that his teaching had helped create leaders who could affect people with their insight and wisdom.

The young priests are in the temple planning its renovation. They scarcely notice that Naibhu's young people have untied him. They bathe his wounds with herbs and heal him. He allows his body to be in their keeping. Naibhu weeps more as he sees their eager faces administering to him as he had many times to them. They bring him food, hold him and they tone together. He is indeed being healed. He sees that his life and struggles have not merely maintained his life but have truly elevated others. He gives thanks to God and the Kuan Yin, who had been with him throughout the cortege beamed with grace.

After he experiences his emotions and is more comfortable, they excitedly tell him about their lives; they are all successful and full of hope for the future. They share with him one of the large problems of their people.

The road which ran through their village had become a main thoroughfare from north to south. The migration of people, loners, families and caravans is constant. They recognize that many people are moving out of desperation and are troubled. Most stop by the temple to find surcease and comfort and to pray. The Hindus rarely enter the temple but did hesitate in the presence of a holy place. His children, now adults, beg him to stay and do his teaching on the steps of their temple as they had seen him do for so many years. This they knew would bring great good to masses of people. They remind him that he would be more successful than the young Buddhic priests inside the temple because Naibhu does not embrace the dogma of either Hindu or Buddhic beliefs and because his radiance attracts people.

Naibhu's heart leaps. Do these young people know that he no longer has a temple, and he had expected to be sacrificed? Probably they do not, but they sense that Naibhu needs a new home to continue his work. Even more significantly, Naibhu needs a place where he can be quiet, with few responsibilities, with more time to expand and enjoy his enlightenment. Some of the teaching of Buddha shared by the old priests had touched him deeply. He desperately wants time to incorporate them into his life and behavior. He realizes that the teachings of the Kuan Yin and the "ancient one" did not address some practical life things that Buddha did to take away the stresses of life and let the person enjoy just living. Naibhu thanks his young friends, but cautiously wonders if the village people will allow that—if the new young priests will let him teach from the steps. Excitedly, they say they will talk with both groups; quickly, they leave to get the answers.

Naibhu at last is alone. Cautiously, he ascends the first temple steps and sits down. He imagines himself greeting the travelers with his warmth and radiance and teaching, not by words but by his shining, expressive countenance. This seems good. He had been moving in that direction at his temple. He sees himself having time to mystically digest some of the Buddhic teachings to ease his compulsive stresses.

The day was closing. The priests have lighted their oil lamps, but are still inside the temple. The travelers have dwindled. The stars are rich and plentiful. Naibhu is at peace. He does not dwell on the future, Buddha taught him this. In the distance he hears toning from many people. Torch lights signal their movement toward him. He knows he will get an answer to his question..."Do your people want me after what I did?" For the first time, he senses not danger or rejection. He knows their answer is yes! Yes! Yes! But of course there are still the temple priests. The toning continues with an occasional interjection of his name. They sit on the steps while a spokesman tells him they want him to be a Senior Priest, "in residence, so to speak." This means he has no temple responsibilities, only community ones with people and travelers as he sees fit. They relay how the people are so touched by his humble confession of his errors and pleading to forgive him that the people have looked at their earlier behavior and realized that they too had erred grievously. They want him in their lives forever and have several fine barns with hay for his home. Naibhu is so choked with emotion he cannot speak only smile, glow and nod his head as he blesses them all. The young spokesman goes on before Naibhu could say, "Yes, but what about the priests?" The young people have solicited the old monks first. They thought it a marvelous idea. They had always been impressed with Naibhu when they saw him working with his people on his temple steps. Their admiration grew during the "mock trial" through his clarity and truthfulness and again as he lay in the cart, injured from the priests' beating and from walking barefoot on a rocky road. They were impressed as they passed the villages where people showed their love for Naibhu and that he did not scream out to them to save him. And most of all, they were deeply affected when he earnestly asked to learn about Buddha and his teachings, and how he talked about his beliefs and how many were the same as Buddha's. They sensed that Naibhu was no ordinary man. He carried some divine presence that was needed in their midst. With conviction they persuade the young priests that he must stay as the priest of the temple steps, to share with his people as they had seen many times before. No words come to Naibhu, only the nod of his head and the tears of joy in his eyes.

That night he does not seek his new hay home. He sleeps on the steps. And the young people who had been his children sleep there with him. They tone and remember with thanksgiving once long ago when his cloak shielded them. Now their grateful love shields him and the entire village. And so he sleeps on the temple steps, not with the raging fires of his pyre, that he envisioned to be built by the priests, but with the twinkling little lights of people to remind him that he is bathed in human and God's lovingness and that his ascension time is now his choice. How simple it is for him to tarry in their midst and watch humans who had glimpsed their destiny grow in divine power. He sees the people reordering their temple as they redirected their lives. He sees their relationships to each other soften as they quietly sense the earth bringing forth abundant crops. He sees their happiness as prevailing. As he senses his destiny, he learns his final personal lesson. He is free now to transcend or work with mankind on the spirit level. And although he is free to cross over, his most beautiful teaching is yet to come. What he had carried in his verbal message, in his acts of kindness, his radiant lovingness must now take a loftier station. Naibhu realizes he is closing a chapter in his life; the recall of his already lived life. By consulting with his memories, he had been listening to his echoes not the real Naibhu. Now he needs to learn about the each-day operating Naibhu.

While he sleeps, his highest self realizes that at last the basis of his life could be unity. Buddha had given him new ways of thinking that freed him from deep cultural bonds and the powerful punishment of self guilt. He knows he will let go of the strong physical attachments to life and live freely. Naibhu as a child knew he was not separated from the animals on the physical earth, now he knows he will never again be separated from anything, including people. His experiences will become fuller as he recognizes that the world is as he experiences it, a flow of vibrations carrying profound and spiritual information. He ´at last knows that his supreme attainment on this earth will be the complete blending of the worldly and the otherworldly, no separation and no opposition. With these thoughts, he sleeps the sleep of expanded enlightenment.

If you were a traveler along that dusty road in eastern India as the years passed, you would have seen the ancient priest Naibhu with flowing white hair and beard set off in a hallowed glow, greeting the travelers from the temple steps. He was available to those who climbed the steps to pray and to those who just hesitated in this sanctified place. He was accessible to all who needed him. He never offered answers to people's problems, but he did show them their place of higher consciousness where they could find complete solutions. For those without strife, he said little but his essence comforted and enlightened everyone. In the late afternoon, he moved quietly among the caravans as they cared for and bedded down their animals. You would see him communicating with the goats as he walked among them. Occasionally, he gave a tender caress to a young brown and black patched one. He recognized all humans and animals as divine creations. At day's end, you could hear his deep resonate voice toning the praise of the day.

The essence of the "beautiful lady" the Kuan Yin, and the "ancient one" were incorporated within his soul as his perfect Yin and Yang. He truly melded divine energy into human form. And the most profound of all was that Naibhu manifested for all to see and know what he was, and he also humbly acknowledged and enjoyed the state he had reached.

May the world bring forth many more magnificent unknown leaders like Naibhu to help guide human destiny while they realize their own.

For Your Enjoyment Additional Discoveries

By
Dr. Valerie Hunt

Enlightening Tapes of Human Energy Fields
Music And Auric Sounds
Color Video With Auric Sounds
And Pictures

Available From

MALIBU PUBLISHING CO.
P.O. Box 4234
Malibu, CA 90264

TEL (310) 457-4694
FAX (310) 457-2717

Music Of Light: Auric Sounds

The world's first authentic sounds produced by the human auric field are harmonically correlated with contemporary, classical and especially composed music. Designed to replenish and make coherent the human energy field. Listeners have described these tapes as a work of art...a magnificent experience associated with feelings of improved vitality and well-being.

STABILIZING
RAINBOW — Progressing in frequency, 13 rich, nourishing and coherent color sounds blend as white light to stabilize the field and encourage broad awareness.

VITALIZING
RED – AMBER – ORANGE — Vibrant stimulating sounds revitalize the physical body and activate spontaneous emotions.

TUNING
YELLOW – GREEN – GOLD — Fine tuning of sensation and perception improves nervous system efficiency and performance and creatively activates the mind.

RELAXING
BLUE – VIOLET – MAUVE — Soothing relaxing spectrum encourages a quiet contemplative state of peaceful higher consciousness.

ELEVATING
WHITE – BLUE – GOLD — Etheric spiritual tones elevate thoughts and imagery to a broader world, richer beauty and deeper wisdom.

COST: 5 Tapes, 60 Minutes Each, DOLBY Stereo
(Not Sold Separately)
Includes Shipping & Handling $150.

Lecture Tapes

INTERNATIONAL HEALING
ENERGY MEDICINE CONFERENCE
Regent's College, England, October 1992
Series by Dr. Valerie V. Hunt, Principal Lecturer

BIOLOGICAL ENERGY FIELD AND ENERGY MEDICINE: INTUITIVE DIAGNOSES

New concepts of the electromagnetic source of life and disease elucidates the current major medical problems: diabetes, sclerosis, fatigue syndrome, viruses, heart and Alzheimer's disease. All point to new diagnoses and treatment modes featuring close cooperation of physicians, psychics and healers.

MIND: THE SOURCE OF PHYSICAL AND EMOTIONAL DISEASES

Major gaps in brain neurophysiology and an emphasis on chemistry with shots and pills to cure all health problems have treated symptoms with limited success and growing danger. Redirected basic research, however, discovers that the mind is a field of information, the true source of all health problems. Energy medicine is the visionary medicine of the future.

FUTURE HEALING: ENERGY FIELD TRANSACTIONS AND CHANGE

Understanding the subtle energy systems that flow through body meridians, connective tissues and by neuropeptide transmission along with discovery of the elegant chaos pattern in the human field makes it understandable why a gentle energy nudge can snatch order out of the random chaos of extensive dysfunction and bring about miraculous healing and regeneration.

COST: 3 Lectures, 4 Tapes, 60 Minutes
Includes Shipping & Handling $50

Video Tape

THE HUMAN ENERGY FIELD AND HEALTH

This video shows for the first time in color the dramatic sounds and pictures of the auric field and documented research slides of Dr. Hunt's amazing energy field findings during health, disease, pain, emotions, imagery and consciousness states.

COST: Color VHS and PAL – 60 minutes
Includes Shipping & Handling $50

Lecture Tape

COLOR PREFERENCES, COLOR NEEDS, COLOR EFFECTS

Color preferences, effects and needs reflect our deepest responses to color. The color vibrations of our own "aura" constitute a color screen which alters and accentuates our visual color perception.

Objects do not possess a fixed color of their own: they only have changing vibrations which result in light reflections from the pigment these contain. It is the reflected light filtered through a person's aura which flavor his judgements to create his physical and emotional experience with color.

Electronic research is discussed as applied to the effects of color upon vitality and strength, relaxation, calmness, and extended sensory awareness.

COST: 90 Minute Tape
Includes Shipping & Handling $16

Lecture Tape

BIOCOSMIC CONNECTION

Research with brain waves, holograms and energy fields is broadly publicized in popular magazines so that many people embrace the philosophical beliefs of the oneness of man and the universe. But we have not known how these two separate material entities actually transact as one and the practical application of these transactions to our lives.

For the first time, pioneering research with high frequency electronics captured and elucidated the human energy field and observed field transactions; people with people, with atmosphere, with Earth vibrations, and with thought waves. From these studies a new model emerged of the macrocosmic links of humans and cosmos, and how the mind-field creates illness and health, underlies all communication and creativity and makes telepathy and clairvoyance rational.

COST: 90 Minute Tape
Includes Shipping & Handling $16

Book

INFINITE MIND:
Science of Human Vibrations of Consciousness
By Valerie V. Hunt

- ❖ Living vibrations validated by electronic frequency research
- ❖ Higher mind discovered to be an energy field throughout the body
- ❖ New models of science and thought pinpoint human energy fields to be the source of all behavior
- ❖ Emotions as energy disclosed to be different at personality and soul levels of consciousness
- ❖ Healing and diagnosis of the frequency patterns of health and disease substantiate Alternative Medicine
- ❖ Mystical connections of higher consciousness found in creativity, healing and spirituality
- ❖ Spiritual connections discovered to occur when human vibrations are elevated and coherent

"Years ahead of its time..."
"A classic you will read many times..."
"A monumental work for everyone's reading..."

COST: Includes shipping & Handling $33.50
CA Residents Add Sales Tax $2.29 $35.79

Book

What Should I Do? *Who Should I Be?*

MIND MASTERY MEDITATIONS
By Valerie V. Hunt

A Book To Help You Discover Your Answers

- ❖ Activates your energy, opens emotions, hastens healing and enhances spirituality
- ❖ Empowers you to live your life with greater ease and success
- ❖ Designed to give you Mastery of your needs, your capacities and your destiny
- ❖ Clear, simple instructions to give you unbelievable skills

COST: Includes shipping & handling $22.95
CA Residents Add Sales Tax $1.56 $24.51

ALL ORDERS

MALIBU PUBLISHING COMPANY
P.O. Box 4234, Malibu CA 90264

TEL (310) 457-4694
FAX (310) 457-2717

U.S. Dollars only – MasterCard, Visa or Personal Check